CRIMINAL JUSTICE

Internship Manual

Margaret L. Brown
Rowan University

Stanley B. Yeldell
Rowan University

Kendall Hunt
publishing company

Kendall Hunt
publishing company

www.kendallhunt.com
Send all inquiries to:
4050 Westmark Drive
Dubuque, IA 52004-1840

Printed in the United States of America
10 9 8 7 6 5 4 3 2

DEDICATION OF LOVE AND DREAMS

This Criminal Justice Internship Manual is dedicated to my late father, Harry F. Brown, and my beloved mother, Margaret M. Brown, who have both loved and encouraged me to pursue all my life's dreams and ambitions, for this I am truly blessed and grateful. And, thank you to Adam Mayer for all your support.

DEDICATION OF INSPIRATIONS

This manual is dedicated to my late mother, Bernice Yeldell, who gave all to me and always found a way for me to continue my desire to succeed within the halls of education.

Moreover, may this text serve as a living testimony to my late wife, Shirley J. Yeldell, whose continued inspiration and belief encouraged me to complete the manuscript with a sense of commitment to the Law and Justice Studies students.

Moreover, may this text serve as a reminder to Doris Sumiel that you can continue to enhance your dream by believing that God is not finished with you.

CONTENTS

ACKNOWLEDGMENTS

We would like to express our appreciation to the criminal justice, security, professional, and criminal justice professors and students who have contributed to this manual, which is richer because of their personal sharing:

Fran Burke, Retired Chief of Police of Washington Twp., NJ and an Adjunct Professor of the Law and Justice Studies Department of Rowan University, NJ

Alan Hart, Former Professor of the Law and Justice Studies Department of Rowan University, NJ; currently Director of the Criminal Justice Department of Burlington County College, NJ

Allan Jiao, Professor of the Law and Justice Studies Department of Rowan University, NJ.

Jennifer Magda, Graduate Law and Justice Studies student at Rowan University, NJ

Raymond Milligan, Retired Chief of Police of Deptford Twp, NJ, and retired Adjunct Professor of the Law and Justice Studies Department of Rowan University, NJ

Anthony Salerno, lated Assistant Professor of the Law and Justice Studies Department of Rowan University, NJ

Heather Van Kleef, Graduate Law and Justice Student Research Assistant of Rowan University, NJ

PREFACE

The Criminal Justice Internship course is a very interesting and diverse vehicle for students to examine the practical aspects of the criminal justice system prior to entering the actual employment arena.

Our interest in this proposed manual evolved from teaching and/or advising criminal justice internship students, over a duration of twenty or more years in the Law and Justice Studies Department at Rowan University. We have discovered there was more than ample need to design and craft a text targeted for the criminal justice students.

Our goal is to formulate and produce a manual that will satisfy the criminal justice market, as well as the political science, sociology, psychology and other disciplines. We envisioned that the manual would be utilized as the primary or required vehicle for criminal justice programs and closely annexed programs.

The students will be able to examine each chapter with simplistic and understanding of how the supporting information will assist the students in guiding them to their desired internship.

The manual solicits the student to actively participate in the learning process rather than the consumption by passive osmosis.

Many of the students will wish to exceed the basic information and utilize the internet and related sources to pursue the internship.

Furthermore, it is our intended goal to produce a multifacet, and versatile manual that will be utilized by professors and practioners within the criminal justice field. Also, we believe two year programs, four year programs and graduated programs will welcome the manual.

It is believed that the students will discover the Internship Manual to be an invaluable road map and an informative resource instrument in their conquest for future employment.

CHAPTER ONE

INTRODUCTION

CHAPTER ONE: INTRODUCTION

This manual will provide the student with a brief introduction to the ever changing fields of the criminal justice system. The manual will serve as a very practical and resource-filled text that includes descriptions and numerous sources for students to select from while in the pursuit of an internship.

Although less than exhaustive in its treatment of competing positions, the manual's comprehensive view assists in clarifying and responding to numerous inquiries about the complexities of internships and their applications to career explorations.

The manual is practically useful as well as theoretically sophisticated, as it includes a meaty description of numerous resources embedded within the context of the manual and available through the internet and networking.

Each chapter reveals the authors' understanding of the integral obstacles, providing plain spoken advice about what it takes to obtain the maximum out-put of an internship; as well as simply to cope with the dynamics of the criminal justice system.

The manual has been crafted so that the basic information or literature can be easily ascertainable during the commencement of each chapter. Moreover, a succinct discussion of the major components of the criminal justice system is coupled with each component's conditions and requirements of employment. The vast opportunities for internships within the criminal justice system include the following criminal justice fields, all of which are covered in this manual: Law Enforcement, Corrections, Courts, Social Justice Organizations and related fields.

The manual consists of ten readable and informative chapters. The manual commences with Chapter One: The Introduction which introduces the theme of the book, with particular attention to the linkage between the major concepts and an overview of the criminal justice system. Chapter Two: Criminal Justice Internships examines the needs an internship fulfills for the student versus the intern's career pursuits and the utilization of the sources, or information. Chapter Three: Educational Requirements articulates agency requirements, formulating learning objectives and the roles of the supervisor and the university faculty advisors. Chapter Four: Internship Portfolio briefly surveys the major components in the formulation of a resume, cover letter and follow-up letter and securing meaningful recommendations. Chapter Five: Law Enforcement Internships describes and analyzes the educational requirements and conditions of employment as they relate to local, county, state and federal and special agencies. Chapter Six: Correctional Internships treats in detail the various levels of correctional institutions and their employment requirements. Chapter Seven: Judicial Internships introduces readers to the systematic levels of the judiciary and the importance of the employment statistics. Chapter Eight: Trends/Visions focuses on how to identify the new emerging fields evolving into the future. Chapter Nine: Criminal Justice Degree Programs lists colleges and universities that offer a bachelor's degree, master's degree and/or Ph.D. program in criminal justice. Chapter Ten concludes the manual with an integrated synthesis of lessons about the need to follow the well crafted road map of an internship program as outlined in this manual.

The standard that must be utilized throughout an internship experience is the reasonable person concept. In the course of an internship, students may encounter complicated interpersonal or institutional matters that are difficult to navigate. The common sense approach mandates the attempt to use these encounters to enhance the student's understanding of complicated matters; the astute student of criminal justice will avoid the obvious pitfalls. The pursuit will foster the learning process so as to develop the student's creative ability and skills, and the real-world experience that an internship provides will extinguish personal prejudice or biases of an important subject matter.

CHAPTER TWO

CRIMINAL JUSTICE INTERNSHIPS

CHAPTER TWO: CRIMINAL JUSTICE INTERNSHIPS

INTRODUCTION

This chapter examines the importance of the internship, what needs it fulfills and how these needs may change according to career pursuits. It then defines the internship and discusses the intent and basic objectives of internship. The chapter provides the student with an immediate challenge by requiring the student to assess his or her own critical needs coupled with how to examine and pursue various careers in the criminal justice field. The impact of technology enhances the student's options for exploring the numerous internships by utilizing the internet research avenues and the invaluable methods of networking.

CHAPTER OUTLINE

1. Defining the Internship
2. Assessment of Needs
3. Career Pursuits
4. Internet Research
5. Networking

DEFINING THE INTERNSHIP

The internships are intended to actively remove the student from the academic classroom and place the intern into a rich blend of environmental and supplemental learning experiences.

The Internship Objectives

 a. Is designed to supplement the formalized classroom theory with a supervised experience within the criminal justice system or related agencies or fields.

 b. Will provide potential employers with the opportunity to observe and examine prospective employees.

 c. Will emphasize an increasing need for field-related experiences and the enhancement of formalized theory through professional training within the criminal justice system.

 d. Will foster a positive link between the university, college or community college and related criminal justice agencies.

 e. Will aid in the determination of the student's career pursuit.

ASSESSMENT OF NEEDS

The internship is the most important experience that the student will encounter during his or her academic career. The student must examine his or her critical needs in order
to decide what internship would satisfy his or her future career goals.

These needs and their internship-related counterparts are as follows:

a. Self-Actualization: Who am I? Opportunity for growth
b. Esteem: Self-worth and self-respect, and promotions
c. Social: Friends and human interaction
d. Security: Safe working conditions, good supervision, job security and training
e. Physical: Good working conditions, rest periods, sufficient income, heating/air conditioning

The internship has the potential to satisfy all five categories of human needs; however, only truly satisfying the internship will actually fulfill every category.

CAREER PURSUITS

The internship is very important in satisfying your needs—not only your financial needs but also your identity and self-esteem needs. For these reasons, it is important to give careful thought to what career you will pursue. This book will help you decide what you want to do with your career. You will have the opportunity to look at what is important to you and what you will have to offer potential employers during the internship.

Choosing a career has never been as difficult as it is today. There are far more occupations than ever before with new ones evolving each and every day.

You must identify your career needs. Examine the list below and rank them according to importance, using one for the most important etc.:

- __10__ Amount of freedom you have on your job
- __5__ Amount of fringe benefits
- __9__ Amount of information you obtain about your performance
- __1__ Amount of employment security
- __4__ Amount of income
- __3__ Amount of praise for a job well done
- __2__ Opportunity for obtaining a promotion
- __6__ Opportunity to participate in making decisions
- __7__ Opportunity to create
- __8__ Opportunity to enhance self-worth or self-esteem

12   Opportunity for development
13   Available resources to complete assignments or projects
11   Respect from others
14   Work environment

INTERNET RESEARCH

The internet will offer a spectacular opportunity to learn about the criminal justice agency or related organizations by accessing the ever increasing number of Web sites. Each site contains valuable information about the sponsoring agency or organizations that offer internship listings.

While these and dozens of other comprehensive sites offer an abundance of internship resources, their usefulness to you depends upon two aspects: 1) the geographical scope of your search; and 2) which area of criminal justice you want to pursue.

It should come as no surprise that a nationwide internship database would not be the most effective instrument if you were hoping to find an internship in your current place of residence, especially if it is not a large urban city. When your search is locally focused, it is not worth spending too much time sorting through thousands of national listings. You can get lucky, of course, but your time would be better spent exploring local resources.

The examination of the Web for criminal justice internship information can be a frustrating task. To ease and expedite this problem, we have assembled a list of Web site addresses that you will find to be very helpful.

NETWORKING

The networking process is a vital and central component of any effective internship search. This procedure will enable the student to continue his or her internship pursuit. Moreover, this will avoid the stop and go cycles of answering newspaper ads and browsing through other periodical resources. The *American Heritage Dictionary* defines networking as:

> An informal system whereby persons having
> common interests or concerns assist each
> other, as in the exchange of information or
> the development of professional contacts

Networking is the practice of utilizing your criminal justice contacts to discover potential internships. Effective networking will give the student an ever-building list of contacts, one of whom will be the individual who may offer you the position for which you have been searching. It can be a tiresome and frustrating process, but it is well worth the effort.

9

There are numerous reasons why some students resist the networking practice. First, some of them view networking as dishonorable because it seems to reward the best searchers rather than the most qualified students. This is a very narrow and self-defeating position. Remember, networking can be the best way to contact that person.

You may be omitting a very important source, your criminal justice professor. The vast majority of individuals who teach criminal justice courses have extensive experience in their chosen fields, often with organizations located near their college or university. You need to ask your professors for advice and names of people to contact. They will be more than happy to assist you.

Another excellent starting point is your college or university's career center. In fact, your college or university criminal justice department may have their own career library. In addition to employment listings, these career centers often collect contact information for alumni who are willing to talk to students about their professions. The most important aspect of this contact is that they have volunteers to speak with students.

Friends and family represent a third source of professional contacts. For example, your Uncle Ted has a very good friend who is a state trooper and that internship intrigues you. You need to pursue this contact and most important, be assertive and respectful; the results may surprise you.

Networking can also help you set up informational interviews, another valuable investment of your internship search time. Informational interviews are less formal talks during which you can ask questions about the agency or the organization. This type of internship exploration has a substantial amount of advantages. First, it will provide to you more information on which to base your career selection. Second, it gives you a chance to articulate your enthusiasm and qualifications to a potential employer even when there are no suitable positions available. Third, an informational interview gives your contact a better sense of your interests and skills, which will help them direct you to other contacts.

Finally, an often-overlooked advantage of networking is that it will help you uncover internships that have not been listed or advertised. Advance information through word-of-mouth is invaluable in giving you a head start over your competition. It not only puts you first in line for consideration, it also shows how resourceful you are. Remember, in order to network effectively, you must be organized. A wide range of products can be very helpful:

1. Day Planner
2. Notebooks
3. Electronic organizers—connections to your computer

Control networking and use it to your advantage and your efforts will result in an ever growing web of people, organizations and related agencies.

CHAPTER THREE

EDUCATIONAL REQUIREMENTS

CHAPTER THREE: EDUCATIONAL REQUIREMENTS

INTRODUCTION

The changing and complex criminal justice system will require enhanced skills and proficiencies. Many will require the interns to possess college degrees and other educational requirements, such as, the completion of sixty-six college-level credits or at least fifteen credits of criminal justice courses.

It is evident that the possession of the college degree will increase your income. Education forms the foundation for the work place. The ever growing professional and technical areas of criminal justice will demand higher capabilities of the applicant. You must acquire new skills to keep up with modern technology. The future will belong to the knowledgeable intern, for one of the many benefits of an internship is that it instills the learner with the concepts called the career learner.

You will find that the different agencies will not have uniform educational standards. Also, the private and public sectors' educational requirements will not be the same.

CHAPTER OUTLINE

This chapter is designed to introduce the students to the essential requirements of completing the internship. The chapter will discuss the following required components of the internship:

1. Internship Syllabus
2. Criminal Justice Agencies' Requirements
3. Internship Application
4. Internship Agreement
5. Supervisor's Role
6. University/College Faculty Coordinator's Role
7. Questions about Internships
8. Supervisor's Evaluation Form
9. Student Assessment Form
10. Internship Research Paper

INTERNSHIP SYLLABUS

The syllabus will articulate the course requirements and the expectations that must be satisfied by the intern. The subsequent criminal intern syllabus serves as an example of the type of form that may be utilized by the university/college faculty/coordinator.

CRIMINAL JUSTICE INTERNSHIP SYLLABUS

1. **Reference Number**:

    a. 21053561 - 3 credits
    b. 21053571 - 3 credits

2. **TBA** (to be announced by Faculty/Coordinator of Internship)

3. **Credits**:   a. Three (3) credits = 150 hours
                     b. Six (6) credits = 300 hours

4. **Pre-Requisites**:

    a. Criminal Law
    ONE OF THE FOLLOWING THREE:
        American Police
        Introduction to Courts
        Introduction to Corrections
    b. Survey of Criminal Justice
    c. Criminal Justice Research
    d. Communication or Composition One and Two
    e. Victimology
    f. Introduction to Computers

5. **Faculty/Coordinator of**
    Internship: _Salem County Sheriff's Department (Doug Bell)_

6. **Course Description**:

    The internship course will serve as the cornerstone of the student's academic experience. The course will remove the student from the academic theoretical classroom and put the student into a rich blend of practical laboratory and experiences yielded by the criminal justice agencies.

7. **Course Objectives**:

    a. The course is designed to supplement the formalized classroom theory with an enriched experience within the criminal justice agencies and related fields.
    b. Will provide potential employers the opportunity to observe prospective employees.
    c. Will emphasize the need for external classroom experiences through internship training.
    d. Will provide the student with an invaluable experience within a practical laboratory.

e.   Will foster a positive linkage between the university or college and the criminal justice agencies.

8. Required Observation:

The student will be required to observe the subsequent integral functions of the criminal justice system:

    a.   Preliminary Hearing
    b.   Grand Jury Proceeding
    c.   Bail Hearings
    d.   Pre-trial Motion
    e.   Roles of the:

        1.   Trial Judge
        2.   Prosecutor or District Attorney
        3.   Public Defender or Defense Attorney

    f.   Arraignment
    g.   Pre-Sentence Investigation Matters
    h.   Discovery
    i.   Plea Bargain Procedures
    j.   Role of Probation
    k.   Law Enforcement Roles in Criminal Cases
    l.   Pre-Trial Alternatives or Diversionary Programs

The previously discussed observational experience does not limit the student to said experiences. There are numerous experiences that have not been cited, but the previous listing will provide the student with the basic foundation of the criminal justice agencies.

9. Course Requirements:

    a.   The student must complete 66 credits (overall) prior to enrolling into the internship course.
    b.   The student must have completed eighteen (18) credits within the major.
    c.   All pre-requisites within four (4) must be completed.
    d.   The students can complete the two internship courses -

        1.   Three Credits = 150 hours
        2.   Six Credits = 300 hours

    e.   Log Book - Loose-Leaf Notebook
        The student must record the following within the book:

1.   Date
2.   Place of Agency
3.   Time of Arrival
4.   Departure Time
5.   Observation - A brief description of his or her daily activities and what was observed.

f.   Learning Objectives

The learning objectives will be put into the research paper. The learning objectives will be discussed with the student's supervisor.

g.   Research Paper

The research paper will be formulated by the university/college faculty/coordinator. The paper must be typed and comply with standard research procedures in writing the paper. The research paper must be submitted by the date required by the university/college faculty/coordinator of internship.

h.   Visitations

The university/college faculty/coordinator will make three (3) on site visits at the criminal justice agency. The visits are designed to serve as a formal contact with the agency:

1.   The first visit will be a meeting with the student and the student's immediate supervisor.
2.   The second visit is to monitor the student's progress.
3.   The third visit is to ascertain the effectiveness of the student's internship.

i.   University/College Responsibilities

1.   The university/college faculty/coordinator serves as the student's advisor and as the link to the criminal justice agencies.
2.   Authorizing students to complete internships without regard to race, religion, sex, age, national origin, or physical handicap.
3.   Briefing the university/college faculty/coordinator regarding the evaluation requirements.
4.   Ensuring that each student receives the educational related internship assignments.
5.   Maintain records of the student internship.
6.   Notification to the university/college faculty/coordinator

that the student intern has been dismissed from the internship because of unsatisfactory performance:
a. Repeated absences without excuses.
b. Failure to complete at least three assignments.
c. Three late arrivals within a semester.
d. General appearance is not acceptable to agency requirements.

j. Student Responsibilities

1. The student must complete all written assignments requested or required by the university/college regarding the internship
2. The student must maintain regular attendance at the criminal justice agency.
3. Repeated absences must be reported immediately to the university/college faculty/coordinator and the supervisor of the criminal justice agency.
4. Fulfilling in a professional manner all the duties and responsibilities assigned by the agency's supervisor.

k. Discharged, Deserted or Dismissed

If the student has been discharged or dismissed by the agency prior to the completion of the internship, the university/college faculty/coordinator will record a No Credit Grade for the internship course.
Also, the student must notify the university/college faculty/coordinator in writing within three days regarding the desertion. The failure to adhere to the previously articulated requirements will result in an automatic "F" grade for said course.

l. Evaluation and Grading

The student will receive an allocated grade of "Pass" or "Fail." The following requirements must be submitted to the university/college faculty/coordinator for the determination of the final grade:

1. The typed research paper
2. The evaluation report completed by your supervisor
3. Log book must be certified by your supervisor
4. The student's assessment of the internship

INTERNSHIP SCHEDULE

The internship schedule will serve as a guide for the students to complete the three (3) credits (150 hours) or the six (6) credits (300 hours) course(s). The student will be required to complete a minimum of ten (10) to fifteen (15) hours per week at the assigned or approved criminal justice agency or related organization(s).

First Week: The Internship Required Checklist

1. Internship Application (see Appendix A)

INTERNSHIP APPLICATION

Please fully complete the following information and write legibly.

Full Name:_____**Social Security #:**_____

School:_____**Date of Graduation:**_____

Major:_____**Minor:**_____

Current status: college junior_____ **college senior**_____ **graduate student**_____

Would you receive course credit for this internship?_____if so, state _____ credits.

Current phone number:_____

Current address:_____
                              street   city, state   zip code

Permanent phone number:_____

Permanent address:_____
                              street   city, state   zip code

Name of faculty/coordinator of internship:_____

Special skills or equipment that you are familiar with:_____

_____

Departments of interest (see Internship Opportunities):_____

_____

Which semester are you applying for: Winter____ Spring___ Summer____ Fall_____

Start date:_____ Ending date:_____

Total number of hours available to work each week: (Maximum 40 hours, five days/week)

Mon._____ Tues._____ Wed._____ Thurs._____ Fri.____ Sat.____ Sun._____

PROSPECTIVE INTERN QUESTIONS

How is my internship application processed once it is received?

A letter of acknowledgement will be sent within three weeks after application deadline. At that point, all resumes will be screened by the agency coordinator and forwarded to the departments that best fit your area of interest, academic course work completed and extracurricular activities. The department supervisor reviews each candidate's resume and will contact those he/she is interested in by telephone.

Should I send my application in early?

Your application should be sent in as early as possible to ensure that all necessary documents are received by the appropriate deadline.

Does all the information in my application need to be sent in at the same time?

No, your recommendation letters may be sent in separately if so stated in your cover letter. However, to be eligible for consideration all required materials must be submitted.

What if my college schedule does not coincide with the internship schedule?

Other arrangements may be made. Please discuss this matter with the departmental intern supervisor when they contact you for an interview.

Is this a paid internship?

Internships are intended to provide a supplemental learning experience to a student's academic studies. Internships do not constitute permanent employment.

What happens after I interview?

A letter of acceptance will be mailed to you if you have been selected as an intern. Please be patient as the interviewing process can be lengthy.

2. Resume

SAMPLE CHRONOLOGICAL RESUME

John Doe

124 Hudson Street
Jacksonville, Florida 32256
JDOE@anyplace.com

CAREER OBJECTIVE

EDUCATION

Bachelor of Arts, Criminal Justice, May 2008

Minor: History

University of North Florida, Jacksonville, Florida
GPA: 3.5, Dean's List

Associate in Arts, Law & Justice, April 2006
Florida Community College, Jacksonville, Florida
GPA: 3.215

INTERNSHIP

Daniel Memorial, Inc., Jacksonville, Florida

Monitor

Summer 2009

- Modeled appropriate and responsible behavior for juvenile youth clients.
- Observed clients' strengths and weaknesses in order to teach independent living skills.
- Assisted with community activities for clients.
- Interacted with doctors, counselors, psychologists and staff on a regular basis.
- Observed individual and group sessions.
- Co-led a group on enhancing self-esteem.

SKILLS

- Software: Windows 95, WordPerfect, Lotus and Microsoft Word.
- Fluent in Spanish.
- Effective team player.
- Possess strong communication skills both orally and written.
- Good leadership skills.
- Able to work with diverse populations.
- Dependable, punctual and reliable.

ACTIVITIES

1997-present

- History Club member.
- African-American Student Union member.

- Chair of Events Committee.
- Co-coordinated a food fund drive for the needy during the holiday season.

1996-present

WORK HISTORY

Chili's Bar and Grill, Jacksonville, Florida.

Team leader and server.

1996-present

- Provide customer service to all dining patrons.
- Promoted to team leader after 6 months of service.
- Train new servers and handle customer complaints.
- Able to fund 50% of college expenses.

J C Penney, Jacksonville, Florida.

Customer Service/Sales Associate.

1994-1996

SAMPLE FUNCTIONAL RESUME

WILLIAM L. SMITH
10 South First Street
Minneapolis, MN 55404
Home Phone: (612) 555-5650

Personal Data: Date of Birth 6-3-62, 6'0", 175 lbs., Single.

Objective:

Position as a law enforcement officer.

Work History:

1987-present Security Officer:	Southdale Shopping Center Edina, Minnesota • Hired as uniformed security officer. Duties include patron assistance, emergency first-aid response, enforcement of property rules and statutes. Assist in training new employees by providing presentations on company rules and state criminal statutes. Frequently appear as witness in court cases resulting from my position. Work with the area law enforcement officers hired to assist during holiday seasons. Act as company representative to Minnesota Loss Control Society.
1985-1987 Officer Worker:	Kenny's Market, Inc. Bloomington, Minnesota • Hired as assistant to the vice-president. Duties included typing, filing and telephone reception. In charge of confidential employee records. Assisted in organizing the company's first loss prevention program.

Education:

1985-1987	BA, University of Minnesota, Minneapolis, Minnesota.
1983-1985	AA, Law Enforcement Certification, Normandale Community College, Bloomington, Minnesota.

| 1986 | Emergency Medical Technical Technician Registration, Hennepin County Vo-Tech, Eden Prairie, Minnesota. |

References available on request.

3. Cover Letter

THE COVER LETTER

You should never submit a resume by itself. All resumes and other documents must be attached by a cover letter, even if it is very brief. You must keep in mind the sequence below when composing the cover letter.

1. Address your cover letter to a specific individual, not an entire organization or division.
2. If you have obtained the recipient's name through networking, be sure to open your cover letter with an acknowledgement of the source (e.g., Dr. Jones suggested you would be an excellent contact person).
3. A cover letter should be brief; limit the letter to a single page.
4. Conduct research about the internship prior to writing the cover letter.
5. Do not restate your entire resume in your cover letter.
6. A cover letter/resume is an employer's first opportunity to evaluate your writing ability.
7. Proofread your letter, carefully.

SAMPLE COVER LETTER INFORMATION

YOUR NAME
YOUR PRESENT ADDRESS
CITY, STATE, ZIP CODE

Date of Correspondence

Name of Individual
Title
Name of company/organization
Address
City, State, Zip Code

Dear Mr./Mrs./Ms. (Last Name):

PARAGRAPH ONE

Tell why you are writing. Name the position, field or general area in which you are interested. Tell how you found out about the position.

PARAGRAPH TWO

Describe your professional/educational qualifications. Cite one or two areas of qualification or experience, which specifically qualify you for the position. Emphasize particular areas of related experience and training. Stress why you are unique, special and the perfect person for the position.

PARAGRAPH THREE

Close by noting that you have enclosed a copy of your resume and that you will provide any additional information requested. Note that you will look forward to a future response and that you would like to schedule an interview.

Sincerely,

Name

AGENCY

BACKGROUND INVESTIGATION FORM
(See Appendix B)

Misrepresentation or misstatement of fact is sufficient cause for the rejection of an applicant or removal from the position._____APPLICANT INITIAL

NAME:_____

ADDRESS:_____

CITY:_____STATE:_____ZIP CODE:_____

ALIAS/NICKNAMES:_____

MAIDEN NAME OR NAME CHANGE:_____

DATE OF BIRTH:_____SOCIAL SECURITY NUMBER:_____

TELEPHONE NUMBER: (H):_____
(Include area code)
                                    (W):_____

E-MAIL ADDRESS:_____

MARKS/SCARS/TATTOOS:_____

    Second Week: The Internship Required Checklist

        1. Internship Coordinator's Letter to Agency(s) discussing required course credits and mandatory hours.

        2. Letter of Confirmation
           The student must obtain letter of confirmation from the agency.

        3. Internship Agreement
           The agreement must be completed by student and agency.

INTERNSHIP AGREEMENT

(See Appendix C)

Between

_____ Department of _____ University or College and

Agency_____.

The _____ Department of _____ University designates
_____ (agency) as an approved internship placement providing a rich blend of
practical laboratory experiences yielded by the criminal justice agency or related agency.

The _____ Department and the _____ Agency commit
themselves to cooperative efforts as described below, in provision of supervised
educational internship experiences for the _____ Department.

This agreement becomes effective on _____, remains in force for a period
_____ of _____ year(s), and renews itself annually, unless either the
_____ Department or the _____ Agency indicates a need for a review
or change.

Any adjustments to the agreement will be included in a written addendum.

In the event of unforeseen circumstances which significantly affect the student's
educational plan, each party with inform the other in writing, so that the appropriate
changes in their agreement may be made within a reasonable amount of time (14 days), to
assure sufficient time for planning.

The _____ Department Agrees To:

1. Work cooperatively with the agency in designing appropriate learning
   experiences and to actively participate with the student and the Internship
   Supervisor or Agency site manager in the decision-making concerning the
   educational appropriateness, timing and the reasonableness of the internship
   experiences.

2. Respect the autonomy of the agency to set its own program as a service
   delivery system.

3. Interview, screen, select and recommend students to be placed at the agency,
   and to make alternate plans for placement of student(s) in the event that such
   planning becomes necessary.

4. Formulate and execute all educational decisions concerning the student, such as: grades, credits, hours completed within the agency and the curriculum in general.

5. Provide consultation to appropriate staff of the agency in the general development of its internship program.

6. The faculty/coordinator of the Internship Program will serve as the Internship Consultant to the agency who will:

   a. Serve as the principal liaison between the department and the agency during each academic semester.

   b. Be available for the agency as need may be concerning the relationships between the agency and the department.

   c. Make periodic visits to the agency to review the student(s) progress.

   d. Discuss policies and procedures of the Internship Course.

7. Provide opportunities for appropriate evaluations of the agency as a setting of student learning.

8. Provide a copy of the department's course syllabus.

The Agency Agrees To:

1. Accept the policy of the department that students are assigned in accordance with the provisions of the Federal Civil Rights Act.

2. Adhere to the objectives of the department as contained in its course syllabus.

3. Accept the conditions stipulated in the course syllabus.

4. Involve the students in meaningful agency programs by utilizing appropriate assignments or tasks.

5. Allow students to use their work product for academic discussion with the Faculty/Coordinator of the Internship Program.

6. Assure that each supervisor or site manager or designated representative will have adequate time within his/her work schedule to:

   a. Satisfy the educational objectives of the students through development of learning opportunities.

b. Prepare for regularly scheduled conferences with students.

c. Meet with the Faculty/Coordinator of the Internship Program at periodic intervals to discuss learning opportunities and student performance.

d. Prepare reports and evaluation as required by the department.

e. Attend appropriate department sponsored meetings or conferences.

7. Permit the use of facilities by students of the department during the period of the placement, including:

a. Space for students in an area sufficiently private for carrying on the assigned work or activity.

b. Clerical services for those records and reports which are produced for the agency.

c. Access to client and agency records as they relate to agency supervision.

8. Assure that the Faculty/Coordinator of the Internship Program is advised of policy and service changes and developments which may affect student learning or the department's curriculum.

9. Inform the Faculty/Coordinator of any early or immediate problems that may develop concerning a student's progress or performance.

10. Provide reimbursement of all student travel expenses on agency business.

11. Observe the University/College calendar with respect to student holiday and vacation periods.

12. Adhere to course objectives:

a. _____

b. _____

c. _____

d. _____

e. _____

FOR THE AGENCY:

_____

_____

BY:_____

DATE:_____

FOR THE:

UNIVERSITY OR COLLEGE

DEPARTMENT

BY:_____

FACULTY/COORDINATOR

OF INTERNSHIP PROGRAM

DATE:_____

4. Waiver and Release Agreement submitted to Faculty/Coordinator of Internship from student.

WAIVER AND RELEASE AGREEMENT
TO FACULTY/COORDINATOR OF INTERNSHIP
(See Appendix D)

I, _____ am a student at _____ University or
_____College, and have agreed to participate in the _____
Department Criminal Justice Internship Program from _____ until _____.
In consideration for being permitted to participate in the program, I hereby agree and represent that:

1. I have or will secure health insurance to provide adequate coverage for any injuries or illnesses that I may sustain or experience while participating in the program. By my signature below I certify that I have confirmed that my health care coverage will adequately cover me during the duration of the program, and hereby release the State of _____, _____ University or _____ College, and the employees and agents of either, from any responsibility or liability for expenses incurred by me for injuries or illnesses (including death) that I may experience during the program.

2. I agree to conduct myself during the program in conformance with course requirements within the syllabus and with policies established by the University or College and agree to be under the authority and supervision of the Internship Coordinator/Faculty member or other University or College approved and designated supervisor.

3. I understand that the University or College reserves the right to decline to retain me in the program at any time should my actions or general behavior, in the sole discretion of the University or College, be determined to impede or obstruct the progress of the program in any way.

4. I understand that, although the University or College has made every reasonable effort to assure my safety while participating in the program, that there are unavoidable risks in travel and other activities that I will undertake as part of my participation in the program, and I hereby release and promise not to sue the State of _____, _____University or _____ College, or the employees and agents of either, for any damages or injury (including death) caused by, deriving from, or associated with my participation in the program, except for such damages or injury as may be caused by the gross negligence or willful misconduct of the employees or agents of the University or College.

5. I agree that, should any provision or aspect of this agreement be found to be unenforceable, that all remaining provisions of the agreement will remain in full force and effect.

6. I represent that my agreement to the provisions herein is wholly voluntary, and further understand that, prior to signing this agreement, I have the right to consult with the Advisor, Counselor, or Attorney of my choice.

7. I agree that, should there be any dispute concerning my participation in the program that would require the adjudication of a court of law, such adjudication will occur in the court of, and be determined by the laws of, the State of _____ .

8. I represent that I am at least eighteen years of age or, if not, that I have secured below the signature of my parent or guardian as well as my own.

Dated: _____

_____
Signature

_____
Name (please print)

Dated: _____

_____
Signature of Parent or Guardian

_____
Name of Parent or
Guardian (please print)

5. Criminal Justice Agency Waiver

WAIVER AND RELEASE AGREEMENT
TO AGENCY
(See Appendix E)

I, _____, am a student at _____ University or
_____College, and have agreed to participate in the _____
Department Criminal Justice Internship Program from _____ until _____.
In consideration for being permitted to participate in the program; I hereby agree and
represent that:

1. I have or will secure health insurance to provide adequate coverage for any
   injuries or illnesses that I may sustain or experience while participating in the
   program. By my signature below I certify that I have confirmed that my health
   care coverage will adequately cover me during the duration of the program, and
   hereby release the State of _____, _____ University or
   _____ College, and the employees and agents of either, from any
   responsibility or liability for expenses incurred by me for injuries or illnesses
   (including death) that I may experience during the program.

2. I agree to conduct myself during the program in conformance with course
   requirements within the syllabus and with policies established by the University
   or College and agree to be under the authority and supervision of the Internship
   Coordinator/Faculty member or other University or College approved and
   designated supervisor.

3. I understand that the University or College reserves the right to decline to retain
   me in the program at any time should my actions or general behavior, in the sole
   discretion of the University or College, be determined to impede or obstruct the
   progress of the program in any way.

4. I understand that, although the University or College has made every reasonable
   effort to assure my safety while participating in the program, that there are
   unavoidable risks in travel and other activities that I will undertake as part of
   my participation in the program, and I hereby release and promise not to sue the
   State of _____, _____University or _____ College,
   or the employees and agents of either, for any damages or injury (including
   death) caused by, deriving from, or associated with my participation in the
   program, except for such damages or injury as may be caused by the gross
   negligence or willful misconduct of the employees or agents of the University
   or College.

5. I agree that, should any provision or aspect of this agreement be found to be
   unenforceable, that all remaining provisions of the agreement will remain in full
   force and effect.

6. I represent that my agreement to the provisions herein is wholly voluntary, and further understand that, prior to signing this agreement, I have the right to consult with the Advisor, Counselor, or Attorney of my choice.

7. I agree that, should there be any dispute concerning my participation in the program that would require the adjudication of a court of law, such adjudication will occur in the court of, and be determined by, the laws of the State of _____.

8. I represent that I am at least eighteen years of age or, if not, that I have secured below the signature of my parent or guardian as well as my own.

Dated: _____

_____
Signature

_____
Name (please print)

Dated: _____

_____
Signature of Parent or Guardian

_____
Name of Parent or
Guardian (please print)

Third Week   The Internship Required Checklist

INTERNSHIP AGREEMENT (See Appendix F)

Between

_____ Department of _____ University or College and

Agency_____.

The _____ Department of _____ University designates
_____ (agency) as an approved internship placement providing a rich blend of practical laboratory experiences yielded by the criminal justice agency or related agency.

The _____ Department and the _____ Agency commit themselves to cooperative efforts as described below, in provision of supervised educational internship experiences for the _____ Department.

This agreement becomes effective on _____, remains in force for a period _____ of _____ year(s), and renews itself annually, unless either the _____ Department or the _____ Agency indicates a need for a review or change.

Any adjustments to the agreement will be included in a written addendum.

In the event of unforeseen circumstances which significantly affect the student's educational plan, each party with inform the other in writing, so that the appropriate changes in their agreement may be made within a reasonable amount of time (14 days), to assure sufficient time for planning.

The _____ Department Agrees To:

1. Work cooperatively with the agency in designing appropriate learning experiences and to actively participate with the student and the Internship Supervisor or Agency site manager in the decision-making concerning the educational appropriateness, timing and the reasonableness of the internship experiences.

2. Respect the autonomy of the agency to set its own program as a service delivery system.

3. Interview, screen, select and recommend students to be placed at the agency, and to make alternate plans for placement of student(s) in the event that such planning becomes necessary.

4. Formulate and execute all educational decisions concerning the student, such as: grades, credits, hours completed within the agency and the curriculum in general.

5. Provide consultation to appropriate staff of the agency in the general development of its internship program.

6. The Faculty/Coordinator of the Internship Program will serve as the Internship Consultant to the agency who will:

   a. Serve as the principal liaison between the department and the agency during each academic semester.

   b. Be available for the agency as need may be concerning the relationships between the agency and the department.

   c. Make periodic visits to the agency to review the student(s) progress.

   d. Discuss policies and procedures of the Internship Course.

7. Provide opportunities for appropriate evaluations of the agency as a setting of student learning.

8. Provide a copy of the department's course syllabus.

The Agency Agrees To:

1. Accept the policy of the department that students are assigned in accordance with the provisions of the Federal Civil Rights Act.

2. Adhere to the objectives of the department as contained in its course syllabus.

3. Accept the conditions stipulated in the course syllabus.

4. Involve the students in meaningful agency programs by utilizing appropriate assignments or tasks.

5. Allow students to use their work product for academic discussion with the Faculty/Coordinator of the Internship Program.

6. Assure that each supervisor or site manager or designated representative will have adequate time within his/her work schedule to:

   a. Satisfy the educational objectives of the students through development

      of learning opportunities.

   b. Prepare for regularly scheduled conferences with students.

   c. Meet with the Faculty/Coordinator of the Internship Program at

      periodic intervals to discuss learning opportunities and student

      performance.

   d. Prepare reports and evaluation as required by the department.

   e. Attend appropriate department sponsored meetings or conferences.

7. Permit the use of facilities by students of the department during the period of the placement, including:

   a. Space for students in an area sufficiently private for carrying on the

      assigned work or activity.

   b. Clerical services for those records and reports which are produced for

      the agency.

   c. Access to client and agency records as they relate to agency

      supervision.

8. Assure that the Faculty/Coordinator of the Internship Program is advised of policy and service changes and developments which may affect student learning or the department's curriculum.

9. Inform the Faculty/Coordinator of any early or immediate problems that may develop concerning a student's progress or performance.

10. Provide reimbursement of all student travel expenses on agency business.

11. Observe the University/College calendar with respect to student holiday and vacation periods.

12. Adhere to course objectives:

     a. _____

     b. _____

     c. _____

     d. _____

     e._____

FOR THE AGENCY: FOR THE:_____

_____   UNIVERSITY OR COLLEGE AND THE

_____   DEPARTMENT

BY:_____   BY:_____

                                  FACULTY/COORDINATOR

                                  OF INTERNSHIP PROGRAM

DATE:_____   DATE:_____

Fifth Week   Learning Objectives

A. The student enrolled in the three (3) credit course must
   formulate five (5) learning objectives:

1._____

2._____

3._____

4._____

5._____

B. The student enrolled in the six (6) credit course must formulate
   ten (10) learning objectives.

1._____

2._____

3._____

4._____

5._____

6._____

7._____

8._____

9._____

10._____

Seventh Week   The student must meet with agency supervisor to discuss
how the following learning objectives are being satisfied:

1. _____

2. _____

3. _____

4. _____

5. _____

6. _____

7. _____

8. _____

9. _____

10. _____

Eighth Week Site Visitation Form (Evaluation completed by internship coordinator)

SECOND VISIT (See Appendix G)

Name of Student_____Title_____

Placement Area_____

Agency Evaluation of the Student Performance

Overall:

Attendance	Excellent ( )	Good ( )	Fair ( )
Reliability	Excellent ( )	Good ( )	Fair ( )
Peer Relations	Excellent ( )	Good ( )	Fair ( )
Supervisory Relations	Excellent ( )	Good ( )	Fair ( )
Understanding of Position	Excellent ( )	Good ( )	Fair ( )
Initiative	Excellent ( )	Good ( )	Fair ( )

Comments_____

_____

_____

_____

The supervisor must certify the number of hours completed by the student:

I,_____ certify that _____
             Supervisor   Student

Has completed _____hours.

Signed_____Date_____
                    Supervisor

This report has been discussed with the student: ( ) YES   ( ) NO

COMMENTS:_____

_____

_____

_____

Tenth Week   The student must itemize all completed projects and tasks.
The itemized list must be submitted to the supervisor.
(See Appendix I)

1. _____

2. _____

3. _____

4. _____

5. _____

6. _____

7. _____

8. _____

9. _____

10. _____

Eleventh Week   The agency supervisor must list and assess the student's completed itemized projects or assignments.
(See Appendix J)

a.) Excellent   b.) Good   c.) Fair   d.) Poor

1._____

2._____

3._____

4._____

5._____

6._____

7._____

8._____

9._____

10._____

OVERALL PERFORMANCE

( ) Outstanding
( ) Very good
( ) Average
( ) Poor

The supervisor must certify the number of hours completed by the student:

I,_____ certify that _____
                    Supervisor   Student
Has completed _____hours.

Signed_____Date_____
                    Supervisor
This report has been discussed with the student: ( ) YES   ( ) NO

COMMENTS:_____

_____

_____

_____

Fifteenth Week   The student must submit the following documents:

☑1. Research Paper ~ /~ *INC*

☑2. Student Log Book ✓

☐3. Student Description of Analysis of Internship Project
   (See Appendix L)   284 .)..   *INC.*

☐4. Exit Letter Forwarded to Agency ~ *INC.*

☐5. Appendix J: Pg~ 297.

☐6. 4 hr. ✓

☐7. 7 hr. ✓

☐8. find Eval ✓

63

CHAPTER FOUR

INTERNSHIP PORTFOLIO

CHAPTER FOUR: THE STUDENT'S INTERNSHIP PORTFOLIO

INTRODUCTION

This chapter is designed to enhance the student's skills in the formulation of a resume and cover letter, and in the organization of a follow-up letter. After reading this chapter, the student will be able to understand the purpose of a resume, the steps to creating a resume and how to prepare for the interview.

Perhaps the most important aspect of formulation of the portfolio is that the student must understand the various types of interviews and how to handle the interview, stress free.

Finally, the student will learn how to close the interviews, how to handle references and recommendations, and how to evaluate reviews of the Intern Performance Rating documents.

CHAPTER OUTLINE

1 The Cover Letter
2. The Formulation of the Resume
3. Types of Resumes

       a. Historical/Chronological Resume
       b. Functional Resume
       c. Analytical Resume

4. Interviews
5. Types of Interviews

       a. Informational Interview
       b. Mass Interviews
       c. Stress Interviews
       d. Courtesy Interviews

6. Closing the Interview
7. The Follow-up Letter

THE COVER LETTER

You should never submit a resume on its own. All resumes and other documents must be attached by a cover letter, even if it is very brief. You must keep in mind the subsequent list when composing the cover letter:

1. Address your cover letter to a specific individual, not an entire organization or division.
2. If you have obtained the recipient's name through networking, be sure to open your cover letter with an acknowledgement of the source (e.g., Dr. Jones suggested you would be an excellent contact person).
3. A cover letter should be brief; limit the letter to a single page.
4. Conduct research about the internship prior to writing the cover letter.
5. Do not restate your entire resume in your cover letter.
6. A cover letter/resume is an employer's first opportunity to evaluate your writing ability.
7. Proofread your letter, carefully.

SAMPLE COVER LETTER INFORMATION

YOUR NAME
YOUR PRESENT ADDRESS
CITY, STATE, ZIP CODE

Date of Correspondence

Name of Individual
Title
Name of company/organization
Address
City, State, Zip Code

Dear Mr./Mrs./Ms. (Last Name):

PARAGRAPH ONE

Tell why you are writing. Name the position, field or general area in which you are interested. Tell how you found out about the position.

PARAGRAPH TWO

Describe your professional/educational qualifications. Cite one or two areas of qualification experience, which specifically qualify you for the position. Emphasize particular areas of related experience and training. Stress why you are unique, special and the perfect person for the position.

PARAGRAPH THREE

Close by noting that you have enclosed a copy of your resume and that you will provide any additional information requested. Note that you will look forward to a future response and that you would like to schedule an interview.

Sincerely,

Name

SAMPLE COVER LETTERS

Heather VanKleef
123 Accounts Payable Lane
Moneyville, NJ 08029
(856) 863-9547

March 19, 2001

Attn: Mr. Mike Vigorita

Personnel Director

Dear Mr. Vigorita,

Anticipating graduation in May 2001, I would like to take this opportunity to express interest in a junior accounting position with your firm upon completion of my academic career.

As an honor student, and recipient of the Medallion Scholar Award for the School Business, I was chosen to intern for the local public accounting firm of Money and Associates, CPA. At Money and Associates, I assisted in the preparation of clients for corporate tax audits, as well as performed intake consultations for tax preparation purposes. My supervising accountant, Mr. Charles Money, was so impressed with my knowledge and performance that he invited me to continue my internship for another semester. On my internship evaluation form he wrote, "Heather VanKleep is a bright and articulate young woman, her knowledge and ability to grasp accounting procedures and principles is quite impressive. I have high hopes for Heather, I believe she will develop into a top-notch accountant. Her willingness to learn and her computer skills set her above the other accounting interns we hired."

With my academic credentials and my current accounting abilities, I would enjoy this opportunity to learn and grow with Coopers & Lybrand as a junior or entry level accountant. Your company has a wonderful reputation and a track record for mentoring accountants. Learning and growing are quite inviting to a graduating senior such as myself.

Enclosed is a copy of my resume, which outlines in detail my credentials. Given this opportunity, I look forward to meeting you for a personal interview. I will be calling you the week of April 29th to arrange a convenient time. I can be reached at (856) 863-9547.

Thank you for your consideration.

Respectfully,

Heather VanKleep

Jennifer Magda

322 Mullica Hill Rd
Glassboro, NJ 08322
(856) 468-6161

March 21, 2001

Doug Funny
Human Relations Manager
Savitz Pharmaceuticals
856 Bozorth Parkway
Esby, NJ 08028

Dear Mr. Funny:

In response to your advertisement in the Glassboro Examiner for the position of salesperson, I hereby submit my letter of application. I was excited when I read your ad since I've had a long-time interest in pharmaceutical sales, and your product line sounds particularly appealing to me.

For the past four years, I have worked as a part-time sales representative for Mary Jane Cosmetics, which has provided me with a wealth of experience in sales, and in research and development. Also, the experience made me confident that I have the personality, assertiveness and persuasive manner required in this line of work. Furthermore, I feel that my past experience and my educational training have prepared me to understand the rudiments of pharmaceutical sales.

Enclosed is a copy of my resume. I would welcome an opportunity to meet with you to discuss my qualifications in further detail. I look forward to hearing from you at your earliest convenience.

Thank you for your time and consideration.

Sincerely,

Jennifer Magda

THE FORMULATION OF THE RESUME

The resume is important to the prospective employer since it will aid the employer in the weeding out of unqualified interns. Also, the resume will help prospective employees cut through a great deal of preliminary questioning about the applicant's qualifications.

The resume is very important to you because it can assist you in getting you into the door for an interview.

The creation of the resume is like crafting a beautiful artistic piece of sculpture. From the commencement of the conception regarding the idea to the completion of the masterpiece, you need to pursue the following specific steps:

1. Secure all relevant information
2. Select the most appropriate type of resume
3. Select a format
4. Compose the initial draft
5. Edit the initial draft
6. Evaluate and revise the resume
7. Print the final draft

SAMPLE OF RESUME CHECKLIST

General resume guidelines

Professional Appearance

☐ Material fits neatly on one page. Margins approximately 1 inch on all four sides. High quality print in black ink.

☐ White or neutral colored paper, 8.5 x 11 inches, 20lb weight. No staples or folds.

☐ Plain font with straight lines, such as Helvetica. Font size 10–14 points.

☐ Bold and capital letters where appropriate for emphasis, but not overdone.

☐ No italics, script, parentheses, brackets, underlining, shading or graphics.

☐ Avoid use of unnecessary punctuation, horizontal or vertical lines.

Format

❑ Name, address, telephone number and e-mail address centered at top, with name in bold or larger font.

❑ Omit extraneous and personal information such as height, weight, age, sex.

❑ Use the format that best suits your needs. Reverse chronological format, listing education and experience from most recent to least recent, is most commonly used.

❑ Objective clearly stating position being sought, usually beginning with "To obtain a position as…." or "Seeking an entry level position in…."

❑ Education category including any college/university from which a degree was earned. GPA, expressed in tenths, may be included if 3.0 or above. Examples in correct format:

Bachelor of Arts, Communication May 2000
Specialization: Public Relations
Rowan University, Glassboro, New Jersey
GPA 3.4, Dean's List

Rowan University, Glassboro, New Jersey expected May 2001
Bachelor of Science, Business Administration
Specialization: Finance
GPA 3.9, Dean's List
Summa Cum Laude Honors anticipated

❑ Experience category including several entries in consistent format:

Job Title   Dates of employment
Company   City, State
Descriptive statements of experience

Content

❑ Job descriptions/accomplishments written in one to five bulleted statements or brief paragraph format, reading in the first person, with pronouns "I" and "me" omitted. Use a variety of action verbs and keyword nouns specific to the major/profession, often the same words used in typical job postings for such a position.

❑ Descriptive statements highlighting skills and abilities, as well as experience and accomplishments. Show evidence of teamwork, computer proficiency, attention to detail, customer satisfaction, willingness to learn new skills, ability to produce results and your enthusiasm/work ethic. Supply enough description to create reader interest but not to overwhelm.

❏ Finished product should be a unique statement about you. It must be professional looking, error free, with consistent verb tense and end punctuation. Do NOT rely on computer spell check, grammar check or resume writing software for your final resume.

TYPES OF RESUMES

There are three basic types of resumes that have been frequently utilized.

HISTORICAL/CHRONOLOGICAL RESUME

The historical/chronological resume is a typical or traditional one often considered to be the most effective. As implied by the name, this style presents information in reverse order, commencing with your recent employment experience and moving back in time to your past employment experience. The education and employment information supports this style. Remember, include the dates and explain any gaps in the chronology.

The historical/chronological resume is easy to read and provides employers with a form that can be quickly read. It is the best format to utilize when remaining in the same field. It is not the best format if you have little related experience.

You should utilize a chronological resume if:

1. You have spent three or more years with previous employers and have not changed jobs frequently.
2. You are seeking a position in the same field in which you have been employed during the course of your career.
3. You have worked for well-known, prestigious companies or organizations.
4. You can show growth and development.
5. Your references are outstanding.

SAMPLE CHRONOLOGICAL RESUME

John Doe
124 Hudson Street

Jacksonville, Florida 32256

JDOE@anyplace.com

CAREER OBJECTIVE

EDUCATION

Bachelor of Arts, Criminal Justice, May 1999

Minor: History
University of North Florida, Jacksonville, Florida
GPA: 3.5, Dean's List

Associate in Arts, Law & Justice, April 1997
Florida Community College, Jacksonville, Florida
GPA: 3.215

INTERNSHIP

Daniel Memorial, Inc., Jacksonville, Florida

Monitor

Summer 1998

- Modeled appropriate and responsible behavior for juvenile youth clients.
- Observed clients' strengths and weaknesses in order to teach independent living skills.
- Assisted with community activities for clients.
- Interacted with doctors, counselors, psychologists and staff on a regular basis.
- Observed individual and group sessions.
- Co-led a group on enhancing self-esteem.

SKILLS

- Software: Windows 95, WordPerfect, Lotus and Microsoft Word.

- Fluent in Spanish.

- Effective team player.
- Possess strong communication skills both orally and written.
- Good leadership skills.
- Able to work with diverse populations.
- Dependable, punctual and reliable.

ACTIVITIES

1997-present

- History Club member.
- African-American Student Union member.

- Chair of Events Committee.
- Co-coordinated a food fund drive for the needy during the 1997 holiday season.

1996-present

WORK HISTORY

1996-present

Chili's Bar and Grill, Jacksonville, Florida.

Team leader and server.

- Provide customer service to all dining patrons.
- Promoted to team leader after 6 months of service.
- Train new servers and handle customer complaints.
- Able to fund 50% of college expenses.

J C Penney, Jacksonville, Florida.

Customer Service/Sales Associate.

1994-1996

FUNCTIONAL RESUME

The functional resume articulates your qualifications and abilities as they relate to the internship you are pursuing. You need to briefly describe your duties and expertise for each job you were employed. This style is advantageous if you have only a few jobs or you have been employed with a specific company or department for a substantial duration. This resume stresses experience and abilities rather than the chronological listing of jobs. It is suggested that you utilize the functional resume if:

1. You are seeking an internship in a new field not related to your present status.
2. You have been unemployed for more than three months.
3. Your duties and responsibilities are complicated and require explanation.
4. You can point to specific accomplishments while on your last two jobs.

SAMPLE FUNCTIONAL RESUME

WILLIAM L. SMITH
10 South First Street
Minneapolis, MN 55404
Home Phone: (612) 555-5650

Personal Data: Date of Birth 6-3-62, 6'0", 175 lbs., Single.

Career Objective:
Position as a law enforcement officer.

Work History:

1987-present	Southdale Shopping Center
	Edina, Minnesota
Security Officer:	

- Hired as uniformed security officer. Duties include patron assistance, emergency first-aid response, enforcement of property rules and statutes. Assist in training new employees by providing presentations on company rules and state criminal statutes. Frequently appear as witness in court cases resulting from my position. Work with the area law enforcement officers hired to assist during holiday seasons. Act as company representative to Minnesota Loss Control Society.

1985-1988	Kenny's Market, Inc.
	Bloomington, Minnesota
Officer Worker:	

- Hired as assistant to the vice-president. Duties included typing, filing and telephone reception. In charge of confidential employee records. Assisted in organizing the company's first loss prevention program.

Education:

1986-1987	BA, University of Minnesota, Minneapolis, Minnesota.
1983-1985	AA, Law Enforcement Certification, Normandale Community College, Bloomington, Minnesota.

1987   Emergency Medical Technical Technician Registration, Hennepin County Vo-Tech, Eden Prairie, Minnesota.

References available on request.

ANALYTICAL RESUME

The analytical resume emphasizes your particular skills. It permits you to stress those skills and talents instead of your work history. The dates are usually omitted, but past jobs and experiences are referred to at some point. You must determine if this approach can best reflect your particular abilities. Finally, the analytical resume is very appropriate if you are changing career goals as it stresses skills and talent instead of past employment.

SAMPLE ANALYTICAL RESUME

WILLIAM L. SMITH
10 South First Street
Minneapolis, MN 55404
Home Phone: (612) 555-5650
Work Phone: (612) 555-9123

Career Objective: Apply my proven ability in loss prevention.

Qualifications:

- Retail Security: Have developed knowledge and skills in the profession while employed as loss prevention officer for several retail stores. In addition to providing undercover and plainclothes loss prevention services as a store detective, have provided extensive training on the subject to store employees. Excellent performance reviews at each position. Continued increases in apprehension statistics. Received "Employee of the Month" award six times for excellent work as a security officer.

- Supervisory Skills: Promoted to supervisor of 17 loss prevention officers at most recent position. Duties included training, delegating duties and scheduling. Performance statistics for the crew increased significantly.

- Organizational Skills: All jobs have required detailed activity reports. Hands-on-experience using computers to organize data. Often provided oral reports to supervisors.

Employers

1983-present   Donaldson's Department Store, Edina, Minnesota.

1982-1983   Tom Thumb Stores, Inc., St. Paul, Minnesota.

1980-1982   Automobile Club of America, St. Louis Park, Minnesota.

Education

1983   Associate of Arts and Private Security Certificate, Normandale
Community College, Bloomington, Minnesota.

Other

1984   Participated in organization of 1984 American Industrial Security
Association National Convention.

References available on request.

INTERVIEWS

The interview has been defined as the formal consultation to evaluate a prospective student or employee's qualifications. The interview is a meeting between the prospective student intern and the prospective agency or organization at which information is obtained and exchanged.

The primary purposes of the personal interview are for the agency or organization to have an opportunity to:

1. Observe you.
2. Listen to you.
3. See how you will perform under stress.
4. Observe your analytical skills.
5. Test your people skills.
6. Test your knowledge.

The interview provides the organization or agency with the opportunity to observe you from a variety of perspectives.

TYPES OF INTERVIEWS

The interviews can be classified as follows:

Informational Interviews

This is the classical interview, where you are asked to come in to the prospective agency or organization; it is an opportunity to examine you regarding the internship. These interviews are straightforward. You have no say about what format your interview will take, so go with the flow. The interview may be formal, relaxed or somewhere in between. Also, you may have only one interview or there may be several.

The formal interview is rather rigid, with questions being asked one after another and the interviewers giving little or no response to tip you off as to how you are doing.

Mass Interviews

The mass interviews involve several candidates being interviewed in rapid succession, or in assembly line fashion. In these situations, the students may blur together in the interviewers' minds and you must pay particular attention to your follow-up to stand out in the crowd.

The mass interviews are assembly line interviews which appear to be difficult on each prospective intern, as well as on those conducting the interviews. The student interns seem to melt together, making it difficult to remember who was who.

This is when it is critical to not only provide a very strong interview, but to also pay attention to your following-up subsequent to the interview.

Stress Interviews

The stress interview is designed to get you to be uptight, so the interviewers can evaluate how you handle stress. Rapid-fire questions, interviewer hostility and unusual furniture configurations may be part of the stress interview. Do not expect these to be comfortable, but they are designed not to be. You cannot do anything about this process, but you should go into the interview with the confidence that regardless of the situation you are confronted with you will do your best.

Courtesy Interviews

The courtesy interviews are done as favors or because of your connections, but they are still legitimate interviewing opportunities and, most important, obtain all you can from this interview.

You have heard the saying, "It's not what you know but who you know." All that matters is that you will have the chance to impress the interviewer. Once you are there, it is all up to you.

CLOSING THE INTERVIEW

You should close the interview on an upbeat note by asking about a starting date or what a typical assignment might be. Never close by asking about money or benefits.

Regardless of the words you choose, make sure the message comes across loud and clear. "I want this internship, and my performance will be outstanding." One of the strongest conclusions a student can ever give to the interviewer is to say, "You'll never regret my internship performance."

Finally, let the interviewer know that you really want the internship.

THE FOLLOW-UP LETTER

The follow-up letter is an excellent opportunity to prove what kind of person you are and increase the possibility of obtaining the internship. You should write your follow-up letter after two or three days have transpired and you have not received any form of communication from the prospective employer.

A follow-up letter should sell you, separate you from your competition and state a next step—such as, "I have a few ideas for the internship that I'd like to discuss with you." The objective is to keep the communication or the dialogue going. The follow-up is one way that student interns self-select themselves into the internship. However, too many letters or calls can just as easily land you in the "NO" pile by identifying you as overly eager or unable to exercise the common sense to know what is too much.

SAMPLE FOLLOW-UP LETTER

Mr. Scott Anderson
1234 Second Avenue
Boulder, CO 23456

July 21, 1999

Protection Plus Security
1234 First Avenue
Denver, CO 12345

Attn: Mr. Ronald Smith,
        President

Dear Mr. Smith:

Thank you for the opportunity to participate in the hiring process for the position of security officer. I delivered my resume to your office yesterday and am sorry to have missed you.

I remain extremely interested in the position and look forward to the possibility of being considered for the job. Please call if you need any further information.

Very sincerely,

Scott Anderson

REFERENCES

If you have advanced to the point where you are being considered for the internship, the organization or agency will want to check your references.

You need to have references that represent a variety of perspectives. You should try to have business, professional, academic and personal references.

Also, you need to select your references carefully. Always ask your referees if they are willing to provide you with a positive reference. Most people do not include references in their resumes. You can say: "References available on request," and prepare a separate sheet of references to make available to prospective employers who request them. This also keeps your references confidential until a request is made for them.

RECOMMENDATIONS

The student should try to secure individuals who will write a meaningful recommendation. The recommendation should not be general in nature, but it should include the following positive characteristics:

1. Specific knowledge that relates to the internship
2. Integrity
3. Motivation
4. Punctuality
5. Confidence
6. Team player
7. Strengths
8. Independence, working alone skills
9. Supervision
10. Skills

REVIEW OF INTERN PERFORMANCE

The faculty/coordinator of the internship course must review the student's performance rating completed by the agency/organization supervisor. The student should request a copy of the supervisor's evaluation and especially the specific comments that earmark the student's strengths. The strengths are documented statements or actual testimonials of the student's capabilities. Also, the student should attach the evaluation to the student portfolio for further references.

CHAPTER FIVE

LAW ENFORCEMENT INTERNSHIPS

CHAPTER FIVE: LAW ENFORCEMENT INTERNSHIPS

INTRODUCTION

This chapter will discuss the largest and most visible component of the criminal justice system—law enforcement. It begins with a brief discussion regarding the conditions and employment outlook in the field, and a brief examination of the various educational requirements. The law enforcement profession is a diverse profession, especially with the recent increase of females and minorities entering the field.

The law enforcement internships consist of the subsequent agencies and programs.

1. Local or municipal law enforcement agencies
2. County law enforcement agencies
3. State law enforcement agencies
4. Federal and special programs

CHAPTER OUTLINE

1. Conditions and Employment
2. Educational Requirements
3. Diversity in the Workforce
4. Females in Law Enforcement
5. Law Enforcement Internships

    a. Local: Chiefs of Police and City Sheriffs
    b. County
    c. State
    d. Federal and Special Programs

CONDITIONS AND EMPLOYMENT

The student must ask the basic question: Is law enforcement for you? The student should make a rationale decision regarding his or her career. Does the student possess the personal attributes needed to be a law enforcement officer? Can you give orders? Can you take orders? Can you remain calm under stress? Can you treat people professionally and apply the law equally? Can you work the hours under the conditions required by the job? Can you control innate and required drives and impulses under various environmental situations, some of which may be ambiguous?

The student needs to be objective or reasonable in rendering decisions that affect an individual's well being.

The future for employment in law enforcement is very positive. It is expected to grow through the 2000's and the field will be broaden with the development of the new and emerging areas.

Unlike some other industries, the need for law enforcement professionals cannot be explained by the simple rules of supply and demand. Within the law enforcement field itself, however, job availability can vary greatly depending on a number of factors, the most obvious of which is a high incidence of crime. We shall see how crime waves change from street crime to technology related offenses—computer and internet offenses.

The projected disparity in the job growth between public and private law enforcement professionals indicates especially increased demand in the private sector. The demand for guards and other private security personnel is expected to increase much faster through the year 2012.

EDUCATIONAL REQUIREMENTS

The large increase of entry levels of law enforcement has been the result of attractive salaries and benefits. The number of qualified candidates exceeds the number of employment openings in federal law enforcement and in most state, local and special departments—programs resulting in the increase of hiring standards and the selectivity by employers. The competition is expected to remain keen for the higher paying jobs with state and federal agencies and municipal law enforcement departments in more affluent jurisdictions.

The federal law enforcement departments are requiring the prospective employees to possess a four-year degree and applicants to the state law enforcement departments must possess a two-year or associate degree.

An example of the FBI Honor Internship Program:

1. Undergraduate students, enrolled in their junior year at the time they apply. Or graduate level students, enrolled in a college or university and attending full time.
2. Students must return to their campus following the program.
3. Must have a minimum 3.0 academic grade point average on a 4.0 scale (or equivalent).
4. Must be a United States citizen or obtain a student visa..
5. Must have personal recommendations of the dean of the university/college or professor.
   head.
6. Must meet other requirements according to the agency.

DIVERSITY IN THE WORKFORCE

The workforce diversity has become a critical issue in law enforcement. The racial and ethnic minorities comprise about twenty-five percent of full-time sworn-in officers in local police departments since the latter part of the 1970's. At the state level, wide variations can be observed along racial and ethnic lines; a more diverse agency can expect greater levels of credibility, respect and confidence from all citizens.

Similar efforts can be observed at the federal level. An excellent example is the United States Secret Service, whose Web site (www.treas.gov/uss) boldly states that the agency is looking for highly qualified men and women from diverse backgrounds. Also, the Bureau of Alcohol, Tobacco and Firearms seeks a diverse workforce that reflects the strength and talents found in the men and women of our nation (www.atf.treas.gov). The FBI goes one step further by placing minority statistics prominently on its special agent employment Web page (www.fbi.gov.).

FEMALES IN LAW ENFORCEMENT

Females represent more than half of the U.S. population but women have experienced minority status in the workplace. This is a reasonable assessment of women in law enforcement, but a positive change has been developing over the last twenty years.

The National Center for Women and Policing released the results of a study regarding females in law enforcement which promotes the increase of females in law enforcement.

> A division of the Feminist Majority Foundation, the National Center for Women and Policing (NCWP), promotes increasing the numbers of women at all ranks of law enforcement as a strategy to reduce police excessive force, strengthen community policing reforms, and improve police response to violence against women. Research

conducted in the United States and internationally demonstrates that women police officers utilize a style of policing that relies less on physical force, are better at defusing potentially violent confrontations and less likely to become involved in use of excessive force, and respond more effectively to violence against women.

A. ADVANTAGES FOR LAW ENFORCEMENT AGENCIES THAT HIRE AND RETAIN MORE WOMEN

1. Female officers are proven to be as competent as their male counterparts.
2. Female officers are less likely to use excessive force.
3. Female officers can help implement community-oriented policing.
4. More females officers will improve law enforcement's response to violence against women.
5. Increasing the presence of female officers reduces problems of sex discrimination and harassment within an agency.

6. The presence of women can bring about beneficial changes in policy for all officers.[1]

B. REMOVING OBSTACLES IN THE SELECTION PROCESS OF WOMEN

The research has shown that women in law enforcement continue to face a variety of obstacles, including negative attitudes, gender discrimination and sexual harassment.

The entry-level selection process possesses a great potential for liability on issues of discrimination. It is very important that the process be thoroughly reviewed to ensure that it is fair and job-related and to avoid the expense and negative publicity resulting from litigation.

C. CHECKLIST FOR REMOVING OBSTACLES IN THE SELECTION PROCESS

The selection process should possess the following checklist:

1. Physical Abilities Test   If the test is likely to have adverse impact on women, a course is given to assist those taking the test to prepare for it.

2. Written Examination   If subject matter experts are utilized to develop areas of questions for written examinations, women officers are included as experts.

3. Structured Oral Interview   Panelists are supportive of employing women as law enforcement officers. Any rater who consistently scores equally qualified women lower than men is

94

removed.

4. Background Investigation	Investigators have been screened for bias against women and other unlawful biases. Investigators have been trained in discrimination and equal employment law.
5. Psychological Examination	The psychologists have been screened for gender bias. The psychologists have been screened for their support of women as law enforcement officers.
6. Medical Evaluation	Medical personnel have been screened for gender bias and any history of improper behavior with patients.
7. Hiring Eligible Applicants	The chief administrator or designee interviews all candidates before making hiring decisions. Older applicants are valued for the life experience they bring to the job.[2]

D. MENTORING TO INCREASE RETENTION

Women often feel isolated when they join the department and have no one to turn to for advice or support, especially in smaller departments. They may eventually lose hope of succeeding in the law enforcement profession without the ability to receive the appropriate guidance. The loss of highly qualified women costs departments significantly in time, training and employee replacement.

Mentoring programs can assist in the retention and promotion of female employees. They can also provide support and encouragement at each critical juncture in a woman's law enforcement career.

Through the pairing of new hires with veteran officers at the beginning of their careers, problems can be identified and resolved early and the transition into the law enforcement culture can be made easier.

The following are Web sites that provide helpful information on developing a mentoring program:

1. Mentoring - a promising experiment in Minnesota.
   http://cyberwerks.com/dataline/agenda/mentormn.html.

2. Police officers for Minority and Women Mentoring.
   http:/www.bayinsider.com/community/groups/pomentoring/

3. Action Mentoring - a workbook

http://www.adinternational.com/adipages/actment.htm

E. PREVENTING SEXUAL AND GENDER HARASSMENT, DISCRIMINATION AND RETALIATION

Sexual harassment is prevalent in most law enforcement agencies. Over the years, various studies have been conducted to determine the extent to which women officers are subjected to sexual/gender harassment.

SOLUTIONS, POLICIES AND PRACTICES

1. Develop a comprehensive sexual harassment policy.
2. Publicize the policy.
3. Design an effective training program.
4. Develop a good training curriculum.

LAW ENFORCEMENT INTERNSHIPS

The subsequent diverse law enforcement internship categories provide the students with an excellent possibility to examine and select the categories of interest.

LOCAL: CHIEFS OF POLICE AND CITY SHERIFFS

ALABAMA

Anniston
1200 Gurnee Ave
Calhoun County 36201
(256) 238-1800

Auburn
141 N Ross St
Lee County 36830
(334) 887-4901

Bessemer
23 N 15th St
Jefferson County 35020
(205) 425-2411

Birmingham
1710 1st Ave N
Jefferson County 35205
(205) 254-1700

Decatur
402 Lee St
Morgan County 35602
(256) 353-2515

Dothan
210 N St Andrews St
Houston County 36303
(334) 793-0215

Florence
702 S Seminary
Lauderdale County 35630
(256) 760-6500

Homewood
1833 29th Ave S
Jefferson County 35209
(205) 877-8637

Hoover
100 Municipal Dr
Jefferson & Shelby Counties 35216
(205) 444-7700

Huntsville
815 Wheeler Ave
Madison County 35804
(256) 427-7001

Madison
100 Hughes Rd
Madison County 35758
(256) 772-5689

Mobile
2460 Government Blvd
Mobile County 36606
(334) 208-1701

Montgomery
320 N Ripley
Montgomery County 36101
(334) 241-2651

Northport
1910 Lurleen B Wallace Blvd N
Tuscaloosa County 35476
(205) 339-6600

ALASKA

Anchorage
4501 S Bragaw St
99507
(907) 786-8590

Fairbanks
656 7th Ave
99701
(907) 459-6500

Juneau
6255 Alaway Ave
99801
(907) 586-2780

ARIZONA

Apache Junction
1001 N Idaho Rd
Pinal County 85219
(480) 982-8260

Avondale
519 E Western Ave
Maricopa County 85323
(623) 932-3660

Bullhead City
1255 Marina Blvd
Mohave County 86442
(520) 763-9200

Chandler
250 E Chicago St
Maricopa County 85225
(480) 782-4000

Flagstaff
120 N Beaver St
Coconino County 86001
(520) 779-3646

Gilbert
1025 S Gilbert Rd
Maricopa County 85296
(480) 503-6500

Glendale
6835 N 57th Dr
Maricopa County 85301
(623) 930-3000

Lake Havasu City
2360 McCulloch Blvd
Mohave County 86403
(520) 680-5403

Mesa
130 N Robson St
Maricopa County 85201
(480) 644-2211

Navajo
PO Box 3360
Window Rock
Apache County 86515
(520) 871-6581

Opelika
501 S 10th St
Lee County 36803
(334) 705-5200

Oro Valley
11000 N La Canada Dr
Pima County 85737
(520) 742-5474

Peoria
8343 W Monroe St
Maricopa County 85345
(623) 773-7096

Phoenix
620 W Washington St
Maricopa County 85003
(602) 262-6151

Phoenix City
1111 Broad St
Russell County 36967
(334) 298-0611

Prattville
101 W Main St
Autauga County 36067
(334) 361-3671

Prescott
222 S Marina
Yuvapai County 86303
(520) 778-1444

Prichard
216 E Prichard Ln
Mobile County 36610
(334) 452-2211

Scottsdale
9065 E Via Linda
Maricopa County 85258
(480) 312-5000

Sierra Vista
911 N Coronado Dr
Cochise County 85635
(520) 452-7500

Surprise
12425 W Bell Rd Ste A105
Maricopa County 85374
(623) 583-1085

Tempe
120 E 5th St
Maricopa County 85281
(480) 350-8306

Tucson
270 S Stone Ave
Pima County 85701
(520) 791-4441

Tuscaloosa
3801 Mill Creek Ave
Tuscaloosa County 35401
(205) 349-2121

Yuma
1500 S 1st Ave
Yuma County 85364
(520) 782-3236

ARKANSAS

Conway
1105 Prairie St
Faulkner County 72032
(501) 450-6126

El Dorado
402 NW Ave
Union County 71730
(870) 881-4100

Fayetteville
100-A W Rock St
Washington County 72701
(501) 587-3555

Fort Smith
100 S 10th St
Sebastian County 72901
(501) 785-4221

Hot Springs
641 Malvern
Garland County 71902
(501) 321-6789

Jacksonville
1412 W Main St
Pulaski County 72076
(501) 892-3191

Jonesboro
410 W Washington
Craighead County 72401
(870) 935-5562

Little Rock
700 W Markham St
Pulaski County 72201
(501) 371-4621

North Little Rock
200 W Pershing Blvd
Pulaski County 72114
(501) 758-1234

Pine Bluff
200 E 8th Ave
Jefferson County 71601
(870) 543-5100

Rogers
1905 S Dixieland Rd
Benton County 72756
(501) 621-1172

Russellville
115 West H
Pope County 72801
(501) 968-3232

Springdale
201 N Spring St
Washington County 72764
(501) 756-8200

Texarkana
100 N State Line
Miller County 75504
(903) 798-3130

West Memphis
626 E Broadway
Crittenden County 72301
(870) 735-1210

CALIFORNIA

Alameda
1555 Oak St
Alameda County 94501
(510) 748-4508

Alhambra
211 S First St
Los Angeles County 91801
(626) 570-5151

Anaheim
425 S Harbor Blvd
Orange County 92805
(714) 765-1900

Antioch
300 L St
Contra Costa County 91007
(626) 574-5150

Bakersfield
1601 Truxtun Ave
Kern County 93302
(661) 326-3800

Berkeley
2171 McKinley Ave
Alameda County 94703
(510) 644-6743

Brea
1 Civic Center Cir
Orange County 92821
(714) 990-7625

Burbank
200 N Third St
Los Angeles County 91510
(818) 238-3200

Chula Vista
276 Fourth Ave
San Diego County 91910
(935) 691-5185

Citrus Heights
6237 S Fountain Square Dr
Citrus Heights 95621
Sacramento County
(916) 874-1015

Compton
301 S Willowbrook Ave
Los Angeles County 90220
(310) 605-5600

Concord
1350 Galindo St
Contra Costa County 94520
(925) 671-3220

Corona
849 W 6th St
Riverside County 91718
(909) 736-2288

Costa Mesa
99 Fair Dr
Orange County 92626
(714) 754-5115

Daly City
333 90th St
San Mateo County 94015
(650) 991-8142

Downey
PO Box 7016
Los Angeles County 90241
(562) 904-2300

El Cajon
100 Fletcher Pkwy
San Diego County 92020
(935) 579-3351

El Monte
11333 Valley Blvd
Los Angeles County 91731
(626) 580-2100

Escondido
700 W Grand Ave
San Diego County 92025
(760) 839-4722

Fairfield
1000 Webster St
Solano County 94533
(707) 428-7300

Fontana
17005 Upland Ave
San Bernardino County 92335
(909) 350-7740

Fremont
2000 Stevenson Blvd
Alameda County 94537
(510) 790-6811

Fresno
2323 Mariposa St
Fresno County 93721
(559) 498-1414

Fullerton
237 W Commonwealth Ave
Orange County 92832
(714) 738-6767

Garden Grove
11301 Acacia Pkwy
Orange County 92842
(714) 741-5900

Glendale
140 N Isabel St
Los Angeles County 91206
(818) 548-4840

Hayward
300 W Winton Ave
Alameda County 94544
(510) 293-7272

Huntington Beach
2000 Main St
Orange County 92648
(714) 536-5902

Inglewood
One Manchester Blvd
Los Angeles County 90301
(310) 412-5200

Irvine
1 Civic Ctr Plz
Orange County 92623
(949) 724-7000

Long Beach
400 W Broadway
Los Angeles County 90802
(562) 570-7301

Los Angeles
150 N Los Angeles St
Los Angeles County 90012
(213) 485-3202

Modesto
601 11th St
Stanislaus County 95353
(209) 572-9500

Oakland
455 7th St
Alameda County 94607
(510) 238-3455

Oceanside
3855 Mission Ave
San Diego County 92054
(760) 435-4450

Ontario
200 N Cherry Ave
San Bernardino County 91764
(909) 395-2090

Orange
1107 N Batavia St
Orange County 92867
(714) 744-7301

Oxnard
251 South C St
Ventura County 93030
(805) 385-7624

Pasadena
207 N Garfield Ave
Los Angeles County 91101
(626) 744-4501

Pomona
490 W Mission Blvd
Los Angeles County 91766
(909) 620-2141

Redding
1313 California St
Shasta County 96001
(530) 225-4211

Rialto
128 N Willow Ave
San Bernardino County 92376
(909) 820-2555

Richmond
401 27th St
Contra Costa County 94804
(510) 620-6655

Riverside
3775 Fairmount Blvd
Riverside County 92501
(909) 826-5321

Sacramento
900 8th St
Sacramento County 95814
(916) 264-5121

Salinas
222 Lincoln Ave
Monterey County 93901
(831) 758-7286

San Bernardino
710 North D St
San Bernardino County 92401
(909) 384-5742

San Diego
1401 Broadway
San Diego County 92101
(916) 531-2777

San Francisco
850 Bryant St Ste 525
San Francisco County 94103
(415) 553-1551

San Jose
201 W Mission St
Santa Clara County 95110
(408) 277-4147

San Mateo
2000 S Delaware St
San Mateo County 94403
(650) 522-7600

Santa Ana
60 Civic Center Plaza
Orange County 92701
(714) 245-8665

Santa Barbara
215 E Figueroa St
Santa Barbara County 93101
(805) 897-2300

Santa Clara
1541 Civic Center Dr
Santa Clara County 95050
(408) 261-5300

Santa Monica
1685 Main St
Los Angeles County 90401
(310) 458-8401

Santa Rosa
965 Sonoma Ave
Sonoma County 95404
(707) 543-3559

Simi Valley
3901 Alamo St
Ventura County 93063
(805) 583-6950

South Gate
8620 California Ave
Los Angeles County 90280
(323) 563-5452

Stockton
22 E Market St
San Joaquin County 95202
(209) 937-8377

Sunnyvale
700 All America Way
Santa Clara County 94086
(408) 730-7160

Torrance
3300 Civic Center Dr
Los Angeles County 90503
(310) 328-3456

Vacaville
630 Merchant St
Solano County 95688
(707) 449-5213

Vallejo
111 Amador St
Solano County 94590
(707) 648-4540

Ventura
1425 Dowell Dr
Ventura County 93003
(805) 339-4400

Visalia
303 S Johnson St
Tulare County 93291
(559) 738-3215

West Covina
1444 W Garvey
Los Angeles County 91791
(626) 814-8501

Westminster
8200 Westminster Blvd
Orange County 92683
(714) 898-3315

Whittier
7315 S Painter Ave
Los Angeles County 90602
(562) 945-8250

COLORADO

Arvada
8101 Ralston Rd
Jefferson County 80001
(303) 431-3050

Aurora
15001 E Alameda Dr
Arapahoe County 80012
(303) 739-6000

Boulder
1805 33rd St
Boulder County 80301
(303) 441-3300

Colorado Springs
705 S Nevada Ave
El Paso County 80901
(719) 444-7000

Denver
1331 Cherokee St
Denver County 80204
(720) 913-6527

Fort Collins
300 Laporte Ave
Larimer County 80521
(970) 221-6540

Greeley
919 7th St Public Sfty Bldg
Weld County 80631
(970) 350-9665

Lakewood
445 S Allison Pkwy
Jefferson County 80226
(303) 987-7111

Loveland
410 E 5th St
Larimer County 80537
(970) 962-2212

Pueblo
130 Central Main St
Pueblo County 81003
(719) 549-1200

Thornton
9500 Civic Center Dr
Adams County 80229
(303) 538-7430

Westminster
8800 N Sheridan Blvd
Adams County 80030
(303) 430-2400

CONNECTICUT

Branford
33 Laurel St
New Haven County 06405
(203) 481-4241

Bridgeport
300 Congress St
Fairfield County 06604
(203) 576-7611

Bristol
131 N Main St
Hartford County 06010
(203) 584-7930

Cheshire
500 Highland Ave
New Haven County 06410
(203) 271-5500

Danbury
120 Main St
Fairfield County 06810
(203) 797-4611

East Hartford
497 Tolland St
Hartford County 06108
(860) 528-4401

East Haven
471 N High St
New Haven County 06512
(203) 468-3820

Enfield
293 Elm St
Hartford County 06082
(860) 763-6400

Fairfield
100 Reef Rd
Fairfield County 06430
(203) 253-4800

Glastonbury
2108 Main St
Hartford County 06033
(860) 633-8301

Greenwich
11 Bruce Place
Fairfield County 06830
(203) 622-8006

Groton (Town of)
68 Groton Long Point Rd
New London County 06340
(860) 445-9721

Hamden
2900 Dixwell Ave
New Haven County 06518
(203) 230-4000

Hartford
50 Jennings Rd
Hartford County 06120
(860) 527-6300

Manchester
239 E Middle Turnpike
Hartford County 06045
(860) 645-5521

Meriden
50 W Main St
New Haven County 06451
(203) 238-1911

Middletown
222 Main St
Middlesex County 06457
(860) 347-6941

Milford
430 Boston Post Rd
New Haven County 06460
(203) 878-6551

Naugatuck
211 Spring St
New Haven County 06770
(203) 729-5221

New Britain
125 Columbus Blvd
Hartford County 06051
(860) 826-3000

New Haven
1 Union Ave
New Haven County 06519
(203) 946-6333

New London
5 Governor Winthrop Blvd
New London County 06320
(860) 447-5269

Newington
131 Cedar St
Hartford County 06111
(860) 666-8445

Norwalk
297 West Ave
Fairfield County 06852
(203) 854-3001

Norwich
70 Thames St
New London County 06360
(860) 886-5561

Shelton
85 Wheeler St
Fairfield County 06484
(203) 924-1544

South Windsor
151 Sand Hill Rd
Hartford County 06074
(860) 644-2551

Southington
351 Main St
Hartford County 06489
(860) 621-0101

Stamford
805 Bedford St
Fairfield County 06901
(203) 977-4681

Stratford
900 Longbrook Ave
Fairfield County 06614
(203) 385-4110

Torrington
576 Main St
Litchfield County 06790
(860) 489-2000

Trumbull
158 Edison Rd
Fairfield County 06611
(203) 261-3665

Vernon
725 Hartford Turnpike
Tolland County 06066
(860) 872-9126

Wallingford
135 N Main St
New Haven County 06492
(203) 294-2828

Waterbury
255 E Main St
New Haven County 06702
(203) 574-6906

West Hartford
103 Raymond Rd
Hartford County 06107
(860) 523-5203

West Haven
355 Main St
New Haven County 06516
(203) 937-3900

Wethersfield
505 Silas Deane Hwy
Hartford County 06109
(860) 571-2900

Windsor
340 Bloomfield Ave
Hartford County 06095
(860) 688-5273

DELAWARE

Dover
400 S Queen St
Kent County 19901
(302) 736-7100

Newark
220 Elkton Rd
New Castle County 19711
(302) 366-7104

Wilmington
300 N Walnut St
New Castle County 19801
(302) 571-4404

DIST OF COLUMBIA

Washington
300 Indiana Ave NW Rm 5080
(202) 727-4218

FLORIDA

Boca Raton
100 NW Boca Raton Blvd
Palm Beach County 33432
(561) 338-1205

Boynton Beach
100 E Boynton Beach Blvd
Palm Beach County 33435
(561) 742-6100

Cape Coral
815 Nicholas Pkwy
Lee County 33990
(941) 574-0699

Clearwater
645 Pierce St
Pinellas County 33756
(727) 562-4336

Coral Springs
2801 Coral Springs Dr
Broward County 33065
(954) 346-1201

Davie
1230 S Nob Hill Rd
Broward County 33314
(954) 693-8200

Daytona Beach
990 Orange Ave
Volusia County 32114
(904) 255-1431

Delray Beach
300 W Atlantic Ave
Palm Beach County 33444
(561) 243-7851

Fort Lauderdale
1300 W Broward Blvd
Broward County 33312
(954) 761-5590

Gainesville
721 NW 6th St
Alachua County 32601
(352) 334-2411

Hialeah
5555 E 8th Ave
Dade County 33013
(305) 953-5301

Hollywood
3250 Hollywood Blvd
Broward County 33021
(954) 967-4300

Jacksonville
501 E Bay St
Duval County 32202
(904) 630-2120

Lakeland
219 N Massachusetts Ave
Polk County 33801
(863) 834-6900

Largo
201 Highland Ave
Pinellas County 33770
(727) 586-7427

Lauderhill
1980 NW 56th Ave
Broward County 33313
(954) 497-4700

Margate
5790 Margate Blvd
Broward County 33063
(954) 972-7111

Melbourne
650 N Apollo Blvd
Brevard County 32935
(321) 259-1211

Miami
400 NW 2nd Ave
Dade County 33128
(305) 579-6565

Miami Beach
1100 Washington Ave
Dade County 33139
(305) 673-7925

Miramar
8915 Miramar Pkwy
Broward County 33025
(954) 431-4600

North Miami
700 NE 124th St
Dade County 33161
(305) 891-0294

Orlando
100 S Hughey Ave
Orange County 32801
(407) 246-2470

Palm Bay
130 Malabar Rd SE
Brevard County 32907
(321) 952-3456

Pembroke Pines
9500 Pines Blvd
Broward County 33024
(954) 431-2200

Pensacola
711 N Hayne St
Escambia County 32501
(850) 435-1855

Plantation
451 NW 70th Terrace
Broward County 33317
(954) 797-2139

Pompano Beach
2601 W Broward Blvd
Broward County 33060
(954) 321-4400

Port St Lucie
121 SW Port St Lucie Blvd
St Lucie County 34984
(561) 871-4111

St Petersburg
1300 1st Ave N
Pinellas County 33705
(727) 893-7539

Sarasota
2050 Ringling Blvd
Sarasota County 34237
(941) 954-7001

Sunrise
10440 W Oakland Park Blvd
Broward County 33351
(954) 746-3363

Tallahassee
234 E 7th Ave
Leon County 32304
(850) 891-4345

Tampa
411 N Franklin St One Police Ctr
Hillsborough County 33602
(813) 276-3200

West Palm Beach
600 Banyan Blvd
Palm Beach County 33401
(561) 653-3401

GEORGIA

Albany
225 Pine Ave
Dougherty County 31702
(229) 431-3277

Alpharetta
2565 Old Milton Pkwy
Fulton County 30004
(678) 297-6306

Atlanta
675 Ponce De Leon Ave
Fulton County 30308
(404) 817-6900

College Park
1871 W Columbia Ave
Fulton County 30337
(404) 761-3131

Dalton
301 Jones St
Whitfield County 30720
(706) 278-9085

East Point
2727 E Point St
Fulton County 30344
(404) 765-1101

Fort Benning
Wold Ave Bldg 215
Muscogee County 31905
(706) 545-1133

Hinesville
123 East M L King Jr Dr
Liberty County 31313
(912) 368-8211

Jonesboro
170 S Main St
Clayton County 30236
(770) 478-7407

La Grange
100 Harrison St
Troup County 30240
(706) 883-2610

Macon
700 Poplar St
Bibb County 31201
(478) 751-7505

Marietta
150 Haynes St
Cobb County 30060
(770) 794-5300

Newnan
54 Perry St
Coweta County 30264
(770) 254-2355

Peachtree City
153 Willow Bend Rd
Fayette County 30269
(770) 487-8866

Rome
5 Government Plz Ste 300
Floyd County 30161
(706) 238-5100

Roswell
39 Hill St
Fulton County 30075
(770) 640-4100

Savannah
323 E Oglethorpe Ave
Chatham County 31412
(912) 651-6664

Smyrna
2646 Atlanta Rd
Cobb County 30080
(770) 434-9481

Summerville
170 Cox St
Chattooga County 30747
(706) 857-0912

Valdosta
500 N Toombs St
Lowndes County 31601
(229) 242-2606

Warner Robins
800 Young Ave
Houston County 31093
(478) 929-1161

HAWAII

Hilo
349 Kapiolani St
Hawaii County 96720
(808) 961-2244

Honolulu
801 S Beretania St
Honolulu County 96813
(808) 529-3161

Lihue
3060 Umi St
Kauai County 96766
(808) 241-6711

Wailuku
55 Mahalani St
Maui County 96793
(808) 244-6400

IDAHO

Boise
7200 Barrister Dr
Ada County 83704
(208) 377-6670

Caldwell
605 Main St
Canyon County 83605
(208) 455-3122

Coeur D'Alene
3818 N Schreiber Way
Kootenai County 83814
(208) 769-2320

Idaho Falls
605 N Capital Ave
Bonneville County 83402
(208) 529-1404

Lewiston
1224 F St
Nez Perce County 83501
(208) 746-0171

Meridian
201 E Idaho Ave
Ada County 83642
(208) 888-6678

Nampa
211 12th Ave S
Canyon County 83651
(208) 465-2257

Pocatello
911 N Seventh
Bannock County 83206
(208) 234-6113

Twin Falls
356 Third Ave E
Twin Falls County 83303
(208) 736-1541

ILLINOIS

Arlington Heights
33 S Arlington Hts Rd
Cook County 60005
(847) 368-5000

Aurora
350 N River St
DuPage County 60506
(630) 801-6500

Berwyn
6647 W 26th St
Cook County 60402
(708) 795-5600

Bloomington
305 S East St
Mc Lean County 61701
(309) 434-2350

Bolingbrook
375 W Briarcliff Rd
Will County 60440
(630) 226-8600

Calumet City
1200 Pulaski Rd
Cook County 60409
(708) 868-2500

Champaign
82 E University St
Champaign County 61820
(217) 351-4567

Chicago
3510 S Michigan Ave
Cook County 60605
(312) 747-5501

Cicero
4932 W 25th Pl
Cook County 60804
(708) 652-2130

Decatur
333 S Franklin St
Macon County 62523
(217) 424-2711

Des Plaines
1418 Miner St
Cook County 60016
(847) 391-5450

Elgin
151 Douglas Ave
Kane County 60120
(847) 289-2760

Evanston
1454 Elmwood Ave
Cook County 60201
(847) 866-5000

Joliet
150 W Washington St
Will County 60432
(815) 724-3201

Markham
16313 Kedzie Pkwy
Cook County 60426
(708) 331-2171

Mount Prospect
112 E Northwest Hwy
Cook County 60056
(847) 870-5656

Naperville
1350 Aurora Ave
DuPage County 60540
(630) 420-6161

Oak Lawn
9446 S Raymond Ave
Cook County 60453
(708) 499-7722

Oak Park
123 Madison Ave
Cook County 60302
(708) 386-3800

Palatine
200 E Wood St
Cook County 60067
(847) 359-9011

Peoria
600 SW Adams St
Peoria County 61614
(309) 494-8300

Rockford
420 W State St
Winnebago County 61101
(815) 987-5839

Schaumburg
1000 W Schaumburg Rd
Cook County 60194
(847) 882-3586

Skokie
Laramie & Main St
Cook County 60077
(847) 982-5900

Springfield
800 E Monroe St #345
Sangamon County 62701
(217) 788-8360

Waukegan
420 Robert V Sabonjian Pl
Lake County 60085
(847) 599-2551

Wheaton
900 W Liberty Dr
DuPage County 60187
(630) 260-2161

INDIANA

Anderson
700 Meridian St
Madison County 46016
(765) 648-6702

Bloomington
220 E 3rd St
Monroe County 47401
(812) 349-3308

Carmel
3 Civic Square
Hamilton County 46032
(317) 571-2500

Columbus
123 Washington St Ste 11
Bartholomew County 47201
(812) 376-2600

East Chicago
4440 Railroad Ave
Lake County 46312
(219) 391-8331

Elkhart
175 Waterfall Dr
Elkhart County 46516
(219) 295-7070

Evansville
15 NW M L King Blvd
Vanderburgh County 47708
(812) 436-7896

Fishers
4 Municipal Dr
Hamilton County 46038
(317) 595-3300

Fort Wayne
1320 E Creighton Ave
Allen County 46803
(219) 427-1230

Gary
1301 Broadway
Lake County 46407
(219) 881-1201

Greenwood
186 Surina Way
Johnson County 46142
(317) 887-5861

Hammond
5925 Calumet Ave
Lake County 46320
(219) 853-6310

Hobart
200 Main St
Lake County 46342
(219) 942-1125

Indianapolis
50 N Alabama St
Marion County 46204
(317) 327-3282

Jeffersonville
501 E Court Ave
Clark County 47130
(812) 283-6633

Kokomo
100 S Union St
Howard County 46901
(765) 456-7100

Lafayette
20 N 6th St
Tippecanoe County 47901
(765) 476-4045

Lawrence
4455 McCoy St
Marion County 46226
(317) 549-6404

Merrillville
7820 Broadway
Lake County 46410
(219) 769-3722

Michigan City
102 W 2nd St
La Porte County 46360
(219) 873-1460

Mishawaka
200 N Church St
St Joseph County 46544
(219) 258-1683

Muncie
300 N High St Ste 215
Delaware County 47305
(765) 747-4822

Munster
1001 Ridge Rd
Lake County 46321
(219) 836-6600

New Albany
311 W First St
Floyd County 47150
(812) 948-5300

Noblesville
135 S 9th St
Hamilton County 46060
(317) 776-6340

Portage
2693 Irving St
Porter County 46368
(219) 762-3122

Richmond
50 N 5th St
Wayne County 47374
(765) 983-7247

Schererville
25 E Joliet
Lake County 46375
(219) 322-5000

South Bend
701 W Sample St
St Joseph County 46601
(219) 235-9311

Terre Haute
17 Harding Ave
Vigo County 47807
(812) 238-1661

West Lafayette
609 W Navajo Dr
Tippecanoe County 47906
(765) 775-2113

IOWA

Ames
515 Clark Ave
Story County 50010
(515) 239-5130

Bettendorf
1609 State St
Scott County 52722
(319) 344-4020

Burlington
424 N 3rd
Des Moines County 52601
(319) 753-8366

Cedar Falls
220 Clay St
Black Hawk County 50613
(319) 268-5150

Cedar Rapids
505 1st St SW
Linn County 52404
(319) 286-5375

Clinton
113 6thAve S
Clinton County 52733
(319) 243-1455

Council Bluffs
227 S 6th St
Pottawattamie County 51503
(712) 328-4701

Davenport
420 Harrison St
Scott County 52801
(319) 326-7778

Des Moines
25 E 1st St
Polk County 50309
(515) 283-4800

Dubuque
770 Iowa St
Dubuque County 52004
(319) 589-4410

Fort Dodge
702 1st Ave S
Webster County 50501
(515) 573-1426

Iowa City
410 E Washington St
Johnson County 52240
(319) 356-5275

Marshalltown
22 N Center St
Marshall County 50158
(515) 754-5725

Mason City
78 S Georgia
Cerro Gordo County
(515) 421-3636

Muscatine
312 E 5th St
Muscatine County 52761
(515) 435-2068

Sioux City
601 Douglas St
Woodbury County 51101
(712) 279-6353

Urbandale
3740 86th St
Polk County 50322
(515) 278-3911

Waterloo
715 Mulberry St
Black Hawk County 50703
(319) 291-4339

West Des Moines
250 G M Mills Civic Pkwy
Polk County 50265
(515) 222-3321

KANSAS

Dodge City
110 E Spruce St
Ford County 67801
(316) 225-8123

Garden City
304 N 9th St
Finney County 67846
(316) 276-1300

Grand Island
211 W 4th St
Fayette County 66103

Hutchinson
210 W 1st Ave
Reno County 67501
(316) 694-2820

Kansas City
701 N 7th St
Wyandotte County 66101
(913) 573-6010

Lawrence
11 E 11th St
Douglas County 66044
(785) 832-7510

Leavenworth
100 N 5th St
Leavenworth County 66048
(913) 651-2260

Leawood
9617 Lee Blvd
Johnson County 66206
(913) 642-5555

Lenexa
12500 W 87th St Pkwy
Johnson County 66215
(913) 477-7200

Olathe
501 E Old 56 Hwy
Johnson County 66061
(913) 782-4500

Overland Park
12400 Foster
Johnson County 66213
(913) 895-6000

Salina
255 N 10th St
Saline County 67401
(785) 826-7210

Shawnee
6535 Quivira Rd
Johnson County 66216
(913) 631-2155

Topeka
320 S Kansas Ave Ste 100
Shawnee County 66603
(785) 368-9551

Wichita
455 N Main St
Sedgwick County 67202
(316) 268-4158

KENTUCKY

Bowling Green
911 Kentucky St
Warren County 42101
(270) 393-4000

Covington
1929 Madison Ave
Kenton County 41014
(859) 292-2222

Elizabethtown
318 S Mulberry St
Hardin County 42701
(270) 765-4125

Frankfort
308 W Second St
Franklin County 40602
(502) 875-8523

Henderson
101 N Water St
Henderson County 42420
(270) 827-8700

Hopkinsville
112 W 1st St
Christian County 42240
(270) 890-1500

Jeffersontown
10410 Taylorville Rd
Jefferson County 40299
(502) 267-0503

Lexington
150 E Main St
Fayette County 40507
(859) 258-3600

Louisville
633 W Jefferson St
Jefferson County 40202
(502) 574-7111

Owensboro
222 E Ninth St
Daviess County 42303
(270) 687-8888

Paducah
1400 Broadway
Mc Cracken County 42001
(270) 444-8590

Raceland
711 Chinn St
Greenup County 41169
(606) 836-8621

Richmond
239 W Main St
Madison County 40475
(859) 623-8911

LOUISIANA

Alexandria
1000 Bolton Ave
Rapides Parish 71309
(318) 441-6401

Baton Rouge
704 Mayflower St
E Baton Rouge Parish 70821
(225) 389-3802

Bossier City
620 Benton Rd
Bossier Parish 71111
(318) 741-8605

Hammond
303 E Thomas St
Tangipahoa Parish 70401
(504) 542-3500

Houma
500 Honduras St
Terrebonne Parish 70360
(504) 873-6300

Jeanerette
1437 Main St
Iberia Parish 70544
(337) 276-6323

Kenner
1801 Williams Blvd
Jefferson Parish 70062
(504) 468-7270

Lafayette
900 E University Ave
Lafayette Parish 70503

Lake Charles
830 Enterprise Blvd
Calcasieu Parish 70601
(337) 491-1311

Monroe
700 Wood St
Ouachita Parish 71201
(318) 329-2600

New Iberia
457 E Main St Rm 104
Iberia Parish 70560
(337) 369-2307

New Orleans
715 S Broad St Ste 501
Orleans Parish 70119
(504) 826-2727

Ruston
401 N Trenton
Lincoln Parish 71270
(318) 255-4141

Shreveport
1234 Texas Ave Rm 8
Caddo Parish 71101
(318) 673-6900

Slidell
2112 Sgt Alfred Dr
St Tammany Parish 70458
(504) 643-3131

MAINE

Bangor
35 Court St
Penobscot County 04401
(207) 947-7384

Lewiston
171 Park St
Androscoggin County 04240
(207) 795-9002

Portland
109 Middle St
Cumberland County 04101
(207) 874-8300

MARYLAND

Annapolis
199 Taylor Ave
Anne Arundel County 21401
(410) 268-9000

Baltimore
601 E Fayette St
Baltimore City 21202
(410-396-2020

Frederick
100 W Patrick St
Frederick County 21701
(301) 694-2106

Gaithersburg
7 E Cedar Ave
Montgomery County 20877
(301) 258-6400

Germantown
20000 Aircraft Dr
Montgomery County 20874
(301) 840-2386

Hagerstown
50 N Burhans Blvd
Washington County 21740
(301) 790-3700

Rockville
1451 Seven Locks Rd
Montgomery County 20854
(301) 279-1591

Salisbury
699 W Salisbury Pkwy
Wicomico County 21801
(410) 548-3165

Silver Spring
801 Sligo Ave
Montgomery County 20910
(301) 565-7740

Wheaton/Glenmont
2300 Randolph Rd
Montgomery County 20902
(240) 773-5500

MASSACHUSETTS

Boston
1 Schroeder Plz
Suffolk County 02120
(617) 343-4200

Brockton
7 Commercial St
Plymouth County 02302
(508) 941-0200

Brookline
350 Washington St
Norfolk County 02445
(617) 730-2249

Cambridge
5 Western Ave
Middlesex County 02139
(617) 349-3378

Chicopee
110 Church St
Hampden County 01020
(413) 592-6341

Fall River
685 Pleasant St
Bristol County 02722
(508) 676-8511

Framingham
1 William Welch Way
Middlesex County 01702
(508) 620-4926

Haverhill
4 Summer St
Essex County 01831
(978) 373-1212

Lawrence
90 Lowell St
Essex County 01840
(978) 794-5900

Lowell
50 Arcand Dr
Middlesex County 01852
(978) 937-3200

Lynn
18 Sutton St
Essex County 01901
(781) 595-2000

Malden
200 Pleasant St
Middlesex County 02148
(781) 397-7171

Medford
100 Main St
Middlesex County 02155
(781) 391-6755

New Bedford
871 Rockdale Ave
Bristol County 02740
(508) 991-6330

Newton
1321 Washington St
W Newton, Middlesex County 02465
(617) 552-7258

Plymouth
20 Long Pond Rd
Plymouth County 02360
(508) 830-4218

Quincy
1 Sea St
Norfolk County 02169
(617) 745-5710

Somerville
220 Washington St
Middlesex County 02143
(617) 625-1600

Springfield
130 Pearl St
Hampden County 01101
(413) 787-6313

Waltham
155 Lexington St
Middlesex County 02452
(781) 893-3707

Westford
53 Main St
Middlesex County 01886
(978) 692-2161

Weymouth
140 Winter St
Norfolk County 02188
(781) 335-1212

Worcester
9-11 Lincoln Sq
Worcester County 01608
(508) 799-8600

MICHIGAN

Ann Arbor
100 N Fifth Ave
Washtenaw County 48104
(734) 994-2848

Battle Creek
20 N Division St
Calhoun County 49014
(616) 966-3322

Canton
1150 S Canton Center Rd
Wayne County 48188
(734) 397-3000

Dearborn
16099 Michigan Ave
Wayne County 48126
(313) 943-2235

Dearborn Heights
6045 Fenton St
Wayne County 48127
(313) 277-6770

Detroit
1300 Beaubien St
Wayne County 48226
(313) 596-1800

East Lansing
409 Park Ln
Ingham County 48823
(517) 351-4220

Farmington Hills
31655 W 11 Mile Rd
Oakland County 48336
(248) 474-6181

Flint
210 E 5th St
Genesee County 48502
(810) 237-6866

Grand Rapids
333 Monroe Ave NW
Kent County 49503
(616) 456-3400

Kalamazoo
215 W Lovell St
Kalamazoo County 49007
(616) 337-8123

Lansing
120 W Michigan Ave
Ingham County 48933
(517) 483-4800

Livonia
15050 Farmington Rd
Wayne County 48154
(734) 466-2400

Novi
45125 W Ten Mile Rd
Oakland County 48375
(248) 348-7100

Pontiac
110 E Pike St
Oakland County 48342
(248) 857-7870

Redford Township
25833 Elsinore
Wayne County 48239
(313) 387-2500

Roseville
29753 Gratiot Ave
Macomb County 48066
(810) 775-2100

Royal Oak
221 E 3rd St
Oakland County 48067
(248) 546-1527

Saginaw
612 Federal Ave
Saginaw County 48607
(989) 759-1229

St Clair Shores
27655 Jefferson St
Macomb County 48081
(810) 445-5300

Southfield
26000 Evergreen Rd
Oakland County 48076
(248) 354-4720

Sterling Heights
40333 Dodge Park Rd
Macomb County 48313
(810) 446-2800

Taylor
23515 Goddard Rd
Wayne County 48180
(734) 287-6611

Troy
500 W Big Beaver Rd
Oakland County 48084
(248) 524-3443

Warren
29900 Civic Center Blvd
Macomb County 48093
(810) 574-4800

Waterford
2303 Crescent Lake Rd
Oakland County 48329
(248) 674-0351

West Bloomfield
4530 Walnut Lake
Oakland County 48325
(248) 682-9200

Westland
36701 Ford Rd
Wayne County 48185
(734) 467-3226

Wyoming
2300 Dehoop SW
Kent County 49509
(616) 530-7309

MINNESOTA

Apple Valley
7100 147th St W
Dakota County 55124
(952) 953-2112

Blaine
9150 Central Ave NE
Anoka County 55434
(763) 785-6125

Bloomington
2215 W Old Shakopee Rd
Hennepin County 55431
(952) 948-3900

Brooklyn Center
6645 Humboldt Ave N
Hennepin County 55430
(763) 569-3333

Burnsville
100 Civic Center Pkwy
Dakota County 55337
(952) 895-4600

Coon Rapids
11155 Robinson Dr
Anoka County 55433
(763) 767-6481

Cottage Grove
7516 80th St S
Washington County 55016
(651) 458-2850

Crystal
4141 Douglas Dr N
Hennepin County 55422
(763) 531-1000

Duluth
City Hall 411 W 1st St
St Louis County 55802
(218) 723-3224

Eagan
3830 Pilot Knob Rd
Dakota County 55122
(651) 681-4700

Eden Prairie
8080 Mitchell Rd
Hennepin County 55344
(952) 949-6200

Edina
4801 W 50th St
Hennepin County 55424
(952) 826-1610

Fridley
6431 University Ave NE
Anoka County 55432
(763) 572-3625

Inner Grove Heights
8150 Barbara Ave
Dakota County 55077
(651) 450-2525

Lakeville
20110 Holyoke Ave
Dakota County 55044
(952) 985-4898

Mankato
710 S Front St
Blue Earth County 56001
(507) 387-8793

Maple Grove
9401 Fernbrook Ln
Hennepin County 55369
(763) 494-6100

Maplewood
1830 E Cnty Rd B
Ramsey County 55109
(651) 770-4545

Minneapolis
350 S 5th St Rm 130
Hennepin County 55415
(612) 673-2853

Minnetonka
14600 Minnetonka Blvd
Hennepin County 55345
(952) 939-8500

Moorhead
915 9th Ave N
Clay County 56560
(218) 299-5141

Oakdale
1584 Hadley Ave N
Washington County 55128
(651) 738-1022

Plymouth
3400 Plymouth Blvd
Hennepin County 55447
(763) 509-5160

Richfield
6700 Portland Ave S
Hennepin County 55423
(612) 861-9800

Rochester
101 SE 4th St
Olmsted County 55904
(507) 285-8300

Roseville
2660 Civic Center Dr
Ramsey County 55113
(651) 490-2255

St Cloud
807 Courthouse Sq
Stearns County 56302
(320) 650-3858

St Louis Park
3015 Raleigh Ave
Hennepin County 55416
(612) 924-2600

St Paul
100 E 11th St
Ramsey County 55101
(651) 291-1111

White Bear Lake
4701 Hwy 61
Ramsey County 55110
(651) 429-8511

Winona
201 W Third St
Winona County 55987
(507) 454-6100

Woodbury
2100 Radio Dr
Washington County 55125
(651) 739-4141

MISSISSIPPI

Biloxi
1045 Howard Ave
Harrison County 39530
(228) 435-6100

Clinton
305 Monroe St
Hinds County 39056
(601) 924-5252

Columbus
115 6th St N
Lowndes County 39701
(662) 328-6206

Greenville
216 Main St
Washington County 38701
(662) 378-1515

Gulfport
2220 15th St
Harrison County 39502
(228) 868-5900

Hattiesburg
#1 Government Plz
Forrest County 39401
(601) 545-4900

Jackson
327 E Pascagoula St
Hinds County 39205
(601) 960-1217

Meridian
2415 6th St
Lauderdale County 39301
(601) 485-1841

Pascagoula
611 Live Oak St
Jackson County 39568
(228) 762-2211

Southaven
8791 Northwest Dr
De Soto County 38671
(662) 393-8654

Starkville
101 Lampkin St
Oktibbeha County 39759
(662) 323-4135

Tupelo
220 Front St N
Lee County 38801
(662) 841-6491

Vicksburg
820 Veto St
Warren County 39180
(601) 636-2511

MISSOURI

Ballwin
300 Park Dr
St Louis County 63011
(636) 227-9636

Blue Springs
1100 Smith St
Jackson County 64015
(816) 228-0165

Cape Girardeau
40 S Spring St
Cape Girardeau County 63703
(573) 335-1635

Chesterfield
184 Chesterfield Industrial Blvd
St Louis County 63005
(636) 537-3000

Columbia
600 E Walnut St
Boone County 65201
(573) 874-7404

Ferguson
222 S Florissant Rd
St Louis County 63135
(314) 522-3100

Florissant
1700 N Hwy 67
St Louis County 63033
(314) 831-7000

Gladstone
7010 N Holmes St
Clay County 64118
(816) 436-2200

Grandview
1200 Main St
Jackson County 64030
(816) 763-3900

Hazelwood
415 Elm Grove Ln
St Louis County 63042
(314) 839-5169

Independence
223 N Memorial Dr
Jackson County 64050
(816) 325-7271

Jefferson City
401 Monroe St
Cole County 65101
(573) 634-6400

Joplin
303 E 3rd St
Jasper County 64801
(417) 623-3131

Kansas City
1125 Locust St
Jackson County 64106
(816) 234-5000

Kirkwood
131 W Madison Ave
St Louis County 63122
(314) 822-5858

Lee's Summit
10 NE Tudor Rd
Jackson County 64086
(816) 969-7380

Maryland Heights
212 Millwell Dr
St Louis County 63043
(314) 298-8700

O'Fallon
100 N Main St
St Charles County 63366
(636) 240-3200

Raytown
10000 E 59th St
Jackson County 64133
(816) 737-6016

St Charles
2645 W Clay St
St Charles County 63301
(636) 949-3300

St Joseph
501 Faraon St
Buchanan County 64501
(816) 271-4700

St Louis
1200 Clark Ave
St Louis County 63103
(314) 444-1212

St Peters
1020 Kimberly
St Charles County 63376
(636) 278-2222

Springfield
321 E Chestnut Expy
Greene County 65802
(417) 864-1782

University City
6801 Delmar Blvd
St Louis County 63130
(314) 862-4555

MONTANA

Bozeman
615 S 16th
Gallatin County 59715
(406) 582-2000

Great Falls
12 1st Ave S
Cascade County 59401
(406) 771-1180

Missoula
435 Ryman St
Missoula County 59802
(406) 523-4777

NEBRASKA

Bellevue
2207 Washington St
Sarpy County 68005
(402) 293-3105

Grand Island
131 S Locust St
Hall County 68801
(308) 385-5400

Kearney
2025 Ave A
Buffalo County 68848
(308) 237-2104

Lincoln
575 S 10th St
Lancaster County 68508
(402) 441-7237

Omaha
505 S 15th St
Douglas County 68102
(402) 444-5600

NEVADA

Elko
1401 College Ave
Elko County 89801
(775) 777-7310

Henderson
223 Lead St
Clark County 89015
(702) 565-8933

North Las Vegas
1301 E Lake Mead Blvd
Clark County 89030
(702) 633-9111

Reno
455 E 2nd St
Washoe County 89505
(775) 334-2175

Sparks
1701 E Prater Way
Washoe County 89434
(775) 353-2220

NEW HAMPSHIRE

Concord
35 Green St
Merrimack County 03301
(603) 225-8600

Derry
1 Municipal Dr
Rockingham County 03038
(603) 432-6111

Dover
46 Locust St
Strafford County 03820
(603) 742-4646

Manchester
351 Chestnut St
Hillsborough County 03101
(603) 628-6137

Merrimack
31 Baboosic Lake Rd
Hillsborough County 03054
(603) 424-4219

Nashua
0 Panther Dr
Hillsborough County 03062
(603) 594-3500

Portsmouth
3 Jenkins Ave
Rockingham County 03801
(603) 427-1500

Rochester
33 Wakefield St
Strafford County 03867
(603) 335-7527

Salem
9 Veterans Memorial Pkwy
Rockingham County 03079
(603) 893-1911

NEW JERSEY

Bayonne
630 Ave C
Hudson County 07002
(201) 858-6900

Brick Township
401 Chambers Bridge Rd
Ocean County 08723
(732) 262-1100

Camden
One Police Plaza
Camden County 08103
(856) 757-7474

Cherry Hill
820 Mercer St
Camden County 08034
(856) 488-7828

Clifton
900 Clifton Ave
Passaic County 07013
(973) 470-5920

Dover Township
255 Oak Ave
Toms River, Ocean County 08754
(732) 349-0150

East Brunswick
1 Jean Walling Civic Ctr Dr
Middlesex County 08816
(732) 390-6917

East Orange
61 N Munn Ave
Essex County 07019
(973) 266-5050

Edison
100 Municipal Blvd
Middlesex County 08817
(732) 248-7421

Elizabeth
1 Police Plz
Union County 07201
(908) 588-2000

Evesham Township
984 Tuckerton Rd
Marlton, Burlington County 08053
(856) 983-1117

Gloucester
1261 Chews Landing
Blackwood, Camden County 08012
(856) 228-4500

Hamilton
1270 White Horse Ave
Mercer County 08619
(609) 581-4016

Irvington
1 Civic Sq Pub Sfty Bldg
Essex County 07111
(973) 399-6507

Jersey City
8 Erie St
Hudson County 07302
(201) 547-5301

Lakewood
231-3rd St
Ocean County 08701
(732) 363-0200

Middletown Township
1 Kings Hwy
Monmouth County 07748
(732) 615-2100

Newark
31 Green St
Essex County 07102
(973) 733-7930

Old Bridge Township
1 Old Bridge Plaza
Middlesex County 08857
(732) 721-5600

Passaic
330 Passaic St
Passaic County 07055
(973) 365-3900

Paterson
111 Broadway
Passaic County 07505
(973) 881-6800

Perth Amboy
351 Rector St
Middlesex County 08861
(732) 442-4400

Piscataway Township
555 Sidney Rd
Middlesex County 08854
(732) 562-2318

Trenton
225 N Clinton Ave
Mercer County 08609
(609) 989-4055

Union
981 Caldwell Ave
Union County 07083
(908) 851-5050

Union City
3715 Palisade Ave
Hudson County 07087
(201) 348-5780

Vineland
111 N 6th St
Cumberland County 08360
(856) 691-4111

Wayne
475 Valley Rd
Passaic County 07470
(973) 633-3588

Wildwood Crest
6101 Pacific Ave
Cape May County 08260
(609) 522-2456

Woodbridge
1 Main St
Middlesex County 07095
(732) 634-7700

NEW MEXICO

Albuquerque
400 Roma Ave NW
Bernalillo County 87102
(505) 768-2200

Las Cruces
217 E Picacho
Dona Ana County 87701
(505) 528-4200

Rio Rancho
500 Quantum Rd
Sandoval County 87174
(505) 891-6770

Roswell
128 W 2nd
Chaves County 88201
(505) 624-6770

Santa Fe
2515 Camino Entrada
Santa Fe County 87505
(505) 473-5010

NEW YORK

Albany
Morton Ave & Broad St
Albany County 12202
(518) 462-8013

Amherst
500 John James Audubon Pkwy
Erie County 14228
(716) 689-1322

Binghamton
38 Hawley St Government Plaza
Broome County 13901
(607) 772-7090

Buffalo
74 Franklin St
Erie County 14202
(716) 851-4444

Cheektowaga
3223 Union Rd
Erie County 14227
(716) 686-3502

Clarkstown
20 Maple Ave
New City, Rockland County 10956
(845) 639-5800

Clay
4483 Rt 31
Onondaga County 13041
(315) 652-3846

Colonie
312 Wolf Rd
Latham, Albany County 12110
(518) 783-2744

Greece
400 Island Cottage Rd
Rochester, Monroe County 14612
(716) 865-9200

Hamburg Town
6100 S Park Ave
Erie County 14075
(716) 649-3800

Hempstead
99 Nicholas Ct
Nassau County 11550
(516) 483-6263

Irondequoit
1300 Titus Ave
Rochester, Monroe County 14617
(716) 336-6000 X:305

Islip Township
401 Main St
Suffolk County 11751
(631) 224-5303

Mount Vernon
Roosevelt Sq N
Westchester County 10550
(914) 665-2500

New Rochelle
475 N Ave
Westchester County 10801
(845) 654-2300

New York City
One Police Plz 14th Fl
New York County 10038
(212) 374-5410

Niagara Falls
520 Hyde Park Blvd
Niagara County 14301
(716) 286-4545

Ramapo
237 Rt 59
Suffern, Rockland County 10901
(845) 357-2400

Rochester
150 S Plymouth Ave
Monroe County 14614
(716) 428-6636

Schenectady
531 Liberty St
Schenectady County 12305
(518) 382-5201

Syracuse
511 S State St
Onondaga County 13202
(315) 442-5250

Tonawanda
1835 Sheridan Dr
Kenmore, Erie County 14223
(716) 879-6607

Troy
55 State St
Rensselaer County 12180
(518) 270-4421

Utica
413 Oriskany St W
Oneida County 13502
(315) 735-3301

Yonkers
104 S Broadway
Westchester County 10701
(914) 377-7200

NORTH CAROLINA

Asheville
100 Court Plaza
Buncombe County 28802
(828) 259-5880

Burlington
267 W Front St
Alamance County 27215
(336) 229-3540

Camp Lejeune
MP Company Hdqtrs Marine Corp Base
Onslow County 28542
(910) 451-3193

Cary
316 N Academy St
Wake County 27512
(919) 469-4022

Chapel Hill
828 Airport Rd
Orange County 27514
(919) 968-2760

Charlotte
601 E Trade St
Mecklenburg County 28202
(704) 336-2337

Concord
30 Market St SW
Cabarrus County 28026
(704) 783-2207

Durham
505 W Chapel Hill St
Durham County 27701
(919) 560-4322

Fayetteville
467 Hay St
Cumberland County 28301
(910) 433-1819

Gastonia
200 E Long Ave
Gaston County 28052
(704) 866-6890

Goldsboro
204 S Center St
Wayne County 27533
(919) 736-4933

Greensboro
300 W Washington St
Guilford County 27402
(336) 373-2450

Greenville
500 S Greene St
Pitt County 27835
(252) 329-4332

Hickory
347 Second Ave SW
Catawba & Burke Counties 28602
(828) 324-2060

High Point
1009 Leonard Ave
Guilford County 27260
(336) 887-7970

Jacksonville
206 Marine Blvd
Onslow County 28541
(910) 455-1472

Kannapolis
314 S Main St
Cabarrus & Rowan Counties 28081
(704) 933-2211

Kinston
205 E King St
Lenoir County 28502
(252) 939-3164

Raleigh
110 S McDowell St
Wake County 27602
(919) 890-3385

Rocky Mount
One Government Plz
Nash County 27804
(252) 972-1471

Salisbury
130 E Liberty St
Rowan County 28144
(704) 638-5344

Wilmington
115 Red Cross St
New Hanover County 28401
(910) 343-3610

Wilson
120 N Goldsboro St
Wilson County 27894
(252) 399-2318

Winston-Salem
725 N Cherry St
Forsyth County 27102
(336) 773-7701

NORTH DAKOTA

Bismarck
700 S 9th St
Burleigh County 58504
(701) 223-1212

Fargo
222 4th St N
Cass County 58102
(701) 235-4493

Grand Forks
122 S 5th St
Grand Forks County 58201
(701) 746-2500

Minot
515 2nd Ave SW
Ward County 58701
(701) 857-4700

OHIO

Akron
217 S High St
Summit County 44308
(330) 375-2244

Canton
221 SW 3rd St
Stark County 44702
(330) 489-3131

Cincinnati
310 Ezzard Charles Dr
Hamilton County 45214
(513) 352-3536

Cleveland
1300 Ontario St
Cuyahoga County 44113
(216) 623-5005

Cleveland Heights
40 Severance Cir
Cuyahoga County 44118
(216) 291-4987

Columbus
120 Marconi Blvd
Franklin County 43215
(614) 645-4600

Cuyahoga Falls
2310 2nd St
Summit County 44221
(330) 928-2181

Dayton
335 W 3rd St
Montgomery County 45402
(937) 333-1082

Elyria
18 W Ave
Lorain County 44035
(440) 326-1200

Euclid
545 E 222nd St
Cuyahoga County 44123
(216) 289-8464

Green Township
6303 Harrison Ave
Cincinnati, Hamilton County 45247
(513) 574-0007

Hamilton
331 S Front St
Butler County 45011
(513) 868-5811

Kettering
3600 Shroyer Rd
Montgomery County 45429
(937) 296-2562

Lakewood
12650 Detroit Ave
Cuyahoga County 44107
(216) 521-6773

Lorain
100 W Erie Ave
Lorain County 44052
(440) 204-2103

Mansfield
30 N Diamond St
Richland County 44902
(419) 755-9724

Mentor
8500 Civic Center Blvd
Lake County 44060
(440) 255-8856

Middletown
1 City Centre Plz
Butler County 45042
(513) 425-7756

Parma
5750 W 54th St
Cuyahoga County 44129
(440) 888-3211

Springfield
130 N Fountain Ave
Clark County 45502
(937) 324-7720

Toledo
525 N Erie St
Jefferson County 43624
(419) 245-3200

Union Township
9113 Cinti-Dayton Rd
West Chester, Butler County 45069
(513) 759-7250

Warren
141 South St SE
Trumbull County 44483
(330) 841-2536

Youngstown
116 W Boardman St
Mahoning County 44503
(330) 742-8923

OKLAHOMA

Ardmore
23 S Washington St
Carter County 73401
(580) 223-1212 X:2527

Bartlesville
100 E Hensley Blvd
Washington County 74003
(918) 338-4001

Broken Arrow
2302 S First Pl
Tulsa County 74012
(918) 259-8404

Edmond
23 E First St
Oklahoma County 73034
(405) 359-4402

Enid
301 W Garriott Rd
Garfield County 73701
(580) 242-7000

Lawton
10 SW 4th St
Comanche County 73501
(580) 581-3200

Midwest City
100 N Midwest Blvd
Oklahoma County 73110
(405) 739-1325

Moore
117 E Main St
Cleveland County 73160
(405) 793-5171

Norman
201B W Gray St
Cleveland County 73069
(405) 366-5201

Oklahoma City
701 Colcord Dr
Oklahoma County 73102
(405) 297-1000

Ponca City
200 E Oklahoma Ave
Kay County 74601
(580) 767-0370

Shawnee
16 W 9th St
Pottawatomie County 74801
(405) 878-1680

Stillwater
723 S Lewis
Payne County 74074
(405) 372-4171

Tulsa
600 Civic Ctr Ste 303
Tulsa County 74103
(918) 596-9328

Yukon
100 S Ranchwood Blvd
Canadian County 73099
(405) 354-1711

OREGON

Albany
1117 Jackson St SE
Linn County 97321
(541) 967-4317

Beaverton
4755 SW Griffith Dr
Washington County 97005
(503) 526-2260

Bend
711 NW Bond St
Deschutes County 97701
(541) 388-5550

Corvallis
180 NW 5th St
Benton County 97339
(541) 766-6924

Eugene
777 Pearl St Rm 107
Lane County 97401
(541) 682-5111

Gladstone
535 Portland Ave
Clackamas County 97027
(503) 656-4253

Gresham
1333 NW Eastman Pkwy
Multnomah County 97030
(503) 618-2313

Hillsboro
205 SE 2nd St
Washington County 97123
(503) 681-6190

Keizer
930 Chemawa Rd NE
Marion County 97303
(503) 390-3713

Lake Oswego
380 A Ave
Clackamas County 97034
(503) 635-0250

Medford
411 W 8th St
Jackson County 98501
(541) 774-2200

Portland
1111 SW 2nd Ave
Multnomah County 97204
(503) 823-0000

Salem
555 Liberty St SE Rm 130
Marion County 97301
(503) 588-6123

Springfield
344 A St
Lane County 97477
(541) 726-3714

Tigard
13125 SW Hall Blvd
Washington County 97223
(503) 639-6168

PENNSYLVANIA

Abington
1166 Old York Rd
Montgomery County 19001
(215) 885-4450

Allentown
425 Hamilton St
Lehigh County 18101
(610) 437-7777

Altoona
1106 16th St
Blair County 16601
(814) 949-2491

Bensalem Township
2400 Byberry Rd
Bucks County 19020
(215) 633-3711

Bethlehem
10 E Church St
Northampton County 18018
(610) 865-7150

Bristol Township
2501 Bath Rd
Bucks County 19007
(215) 785-4052

Erie
626 State St
Erie County 16501
(814) 870-1125

Harrisburg
123 Walnut St
Dauphin County 17101
(717) 255-3131

Haverford Township
Darby & Manoa Rd
Havertown, Delaware County 19083
(610) 853-1104

Lancaster
39 E Chestnut St
Lancaster County 17602
(717) 291-4911

Lower Merion Township
71 E Lancaster
Ardmore, Montgomery County 19003

Millcreek Township
3608 W 26th St
Erie, Erie County 16506
(814) 833-7777

Penn Hills
12245 Frankstown Rd
Penn Hills, Allegheny County 15235
(412) 793-1000

Philadelphia
8th & Race St Franklin Sq
Philadelphia County 19106
(215) 686-3280

Pittsburgh
100 Grant St
Allegheny County 15219
(412) 255-2814

Reading
815 Washington St
Berks County 19601
(610) 655-6241

Scranton
340 N Washington Ave
Lackawanna County 18503
(570) 348-4130

State College
118 S Fraser St
Centre County 16801
(814) 234-7150

Upper Darby Township
7236 W Chester Pike
Delaware County 19082
(610) 734-7686

RHODE ISLAND

Coventry
1075 Main St
Kent County 02816
(401) 826-1100

Cranston
275 Atwood Ave
Providence County 02920
(401) 942-2211

Cumberland
1380 Diamond Hill Rd
Providence County 02864
(401) 333-2500

East Providence
750 Waterman Ave
Providence County 02914
(401) 435-7600

Johnston
1651 Atwood Ave
Providence County 02919
(401) 231-4210

Lincoln
100 Old River Rd
Providence County 02865
(401) 333-1111

Newport
120 Broadway
Newport County 02840
(401) 847-1306

North Providence
1967 Mineral Spring Ave
Providence County 02904
(401) 231-4533

Pawtucket
121 Roosevelt Ave
Providence County 02860
(401) 727-9100

Providence
209 Fountain St Rm 309 3rd Fl
Providence County 02903
(401) 272-3121

Warwick
99 Veterans Memorial Dr
Kent County 02886
(401) 468-4200

West Warwick
1162 Main St
Kent County 02893
(401) 822-9234

Westerly
5 Union St
Washington County 02891
(401) 596-2022

Woonsocket
242 Clinton St
Providence County 02895
(401) 766-1212

SOUTH CAROLINA

Aiken
251 Laurnes
Aiken County 29801
(803) 642-7620

Anderson
401 S Main St
Anderson County 29624
(864) 231-2280

Charleston
180 Lockwood Blvd
Charleston County 29403
(843) 720-2400

Columbia
1 Justice Square
Richland County 29201
(803) 733-8409

Florence
180 N Irby ST
Florence County 29501
(843) 676-8800

Goose Creek
519 N Goose Creek Blvd
Berkeley County 29445
(843) 863-5200

Greenville
4 McGee St
Greenville County 29601
(864) 467-5310

Greenwood
520 Monument St
Greenwood County 29648
(864) 942-8401

Mount Pleasant
100 Ann Edwards Ln
Charleston County 29464
(843) 884-4176

Myrtle Beach
1101 Oak St
Horry County 29577
(843) 918-1300

North Charleston
4900 LaCross Rd
Charleston County 29419
(843) 740-2831

Rock Hill
120 E Black St
York County 29730
(803) 329 7200

Spartanburg
145 Broad St
Spartanburg County 29306
(864) 596-2376

Summerville
300 W 2nd N St
Dorchester County 29483
(843) 851-4100

Sumter
107 E Hampton Ave
Sumter County 29150
(803) 773-1561

SOUTH DAKOTA

Aberdeen
123 S Lincoln St
Brown County 57401
(605) 626-7000

Rapid City
300 Kansas City St
Pennington County 57701
(605) 394-4133

Sioux Falls
500 N Minnesota Ave
Minnehaha County 57104
(605) 367-7212

TENNESSEE

Bartlett
3730 Appling Rd
Shelby County 38133
(901) 385-5566

Chattanooga
3300 Amnicola Hwy
Hamilton County 37406
(423) 698-9662

Clarksville
701 Red River Rd
Montgomery County 37040
(931) 553-2402

Cleveland
163 1st St NE
Bradley County 37311
(423) 559-3311

Collierville
156 N Rowlett St
Shelby County 38017
(901) 853-3211

Columbia
800 Westover Dr
Maury County 38401
(931) 380-2720

Cookeville
10 E Broad St
Putnam County 38503
(931) 526-2125

Germantown
1930 S Germantown Rd
Shelby County 38183
(901) 757-7300

Hendersonville
3 Executive Park Dr
Sumner County 37075
(615) 822-1111

Jackson
234 Institute St
Madison County 38301
(901) 425-8400

Johnson City
601 E Main St
Washington County 37605
(423) 434-6159

Kingsport
200 Shelby St
Sullivan County 37660
(423) 229-9423

Knoxville
800 E Church Ave
Knox County 37927
(865) 521-1229

Memphis
201 Poplar Ave St 12-05
Shelby County 38103
(901) 545-5700

Murfreesboro
302 S Church St
Rutherford County 37130
(615) 849-2673

Nashville
200 James Robertson Pkwy
Davidson County 37201
(615) 862-7400

Oak Ridge
200 S Tulane Ave
Anderson County 37830
(865) 482-8404

Smyrna
315 S Lowry St
Rutherford County 37167
(615) 459-6644

TEXAS

Abilene
450 Pecan
Taylor County 79602
(915) 676-6600

Amarillo
200 SE Third Ave
Potter County 79101
(806) 378-4261

Arlington
620 W Division St
Tarrant County 76004
(817) 459-700

Baytown
3200 N Main St
Harris County 77521
(281) 422-8371

Beaumont
255 College
Jefferson County 77704
(409) 880-3801

Bedford
2121 L Don Dodson Dr
Tarrant County 76021
(817) 952-2400

Brownsville
600 E Jackson St
Cameron County 78520
(956) 548-7050

Bryan
301 S Texas
Brazos County 77805
(979) 822-0078

Carrollton
2025 Jackson Rd
Dallas County 75006
(972) 466-3290

College Station
2611 A Texas Ave
Brazos County 77840
(979) 764-3600

Corpus Christi
321 John Sartain St Rm 525
Nueces County 78469
(361) 886-2600

Dallas
2014 Main St Rm 506
Dallas County 75201
(214) 670-4402

Denton
601 E Hickory St Ste E
Denton County 76205
(940) 349-8181

El Paso
911 N Raynor St
El Paso County 79903
(915) 564-7309

Fort Worth
350 W Belknap St
Tarrant County 76102
(817) 877-8385

Galveston
2517 Ave H
Galveston County 77550
(409) 766-2100

Garland
217 N 5th St
Dallas County 75040
(972) 205-2011

Grand Prairie
801 Conover Dr
Dallas County 75051
(972) 237-8710

Houston
1200 Travis 16th Fl
Harris County 77002
(713) 308-1600

Irving
305 N O'Connor
Dallas County 75061
(972) 721-2650

Killeen
402 N 2nd St
Bell County 76541
(254) 526-8311

Laredo
4712 Maher Ave
Webb County 78041
(956) 795-2899

Lewisville
184 N Valley Pkwy
Denton County 75067
(972) 219-3611

Longview
302 W Cotton
Gregg County 75601
(903) 237-1199

Mc Allen
1501 W Pecan Blvd
Hidalgo County 78501
(956) 972-7315

Mesquite
711 N Galloway Ave
Dallas County 75149
(972) 216-6228

Midland
601 N Loraine St
Midland County 79702
(915) 685-7103

North Richland Hills
7301 NE Loop 820
Tarrant County 76180
(817) 427-7000

Odessa
205 N Grant Ave
Ector County 79761
(915) 335-3335

Pasadena
1114 Jeff Ginn Memorial Dr
Harris County 77506
(713) 477-1221

Plano
PO Box 860358
Collin County 75086
(972) 424-5678

Port Arthur
645-4th St
Jefferson County 77640
(409) 983-8613

Richardson
140 N Greenville
Dallas County 75081
(972) 238-3800

Round Rock
615 E Palm Valley Blvd
Williamson County 78664
(512) 218-5500

San Angelo
401 E Beauregard St
Tom Green County 76903
(915) 657-4336

San Antonio
214 W Nueva St
Bexar County 78207
(210) 207-7484

Sugar Land
1200 Hwy 6
Fort Bend County 77487
(281) 275-2500

Temple
105 S 5th St
Bell County 76501
(254) 298-5536

Tyler
711 W Ferguson St
Smith County 75702
(903) 531-1015

Victoria
306 S Bridge St
Victoria County 77901
(361) 572-2727

Waco
721 N 4th
Mc Lennan County 76701
(254) 750-7500

Wichita Falls
610 Holiday St
Wichita County 76301
(940) 761-7733

UTAH

Bountiful
805 S Main St
Davis County 84010
(801) 298-6000

Clearfield
55 S State St
Davis County 84015
(801) 774-7240

Layton
429 Wasatch Dr
Davis County 84041
(801) 497-8300

Logan
45 W 200 N
Cache County 84321
(435-750-9900

Midvale
655 W Center St
Salt Lake County 84047
(801) 567-7250

Murray
5025 S State St
Salt Lake County 84107
(801) 264-2673

Ogden
2186 Lincoln Ave
Weber County 84401
(801) 629-8226

Orem
26 N State St
Utah County 84057
(801) 229-7062

Pleasant Grove
87 E 100 S
Utah County 84062
(801) 785-3506

Provo
48 S 300 W
Utah County 84603
(801) 852-6200

Roy City
5051 S 1900 W
Weber County 84067
(801) 774-1010

St George
265 N 200 E
Washington County 84770
(435) 634-5001

Salt Lake City
315 E 200 S
Salt Lake County 84111
(801) 799-3000

Sandy
10000 S Centennial Pkwy
Salt Lake County 84070
(801) 568-7214

South Jordan
11175 S Redwood Rd
Salt Lake County 84095
(801) 254-4708

West Jordan
8000 S Redwood Rd
Salt Lake County 84088
(801) 569-5200

West Valley City
3600 S Constitution Blvd
Salt Lake County 84119
(801) 963-3300

VERMONT

Burlington
1 North Ave
Chittenden County 05401
(802) 658-2700

VIRGINIA

Alexandria
2003 Mill Rd
22314
(703) 838-4114

Blacksburg
200 Clay St SW
Montgomery County 24060
(540) 961-1152

Charlottesville
315 E High St
22902
(804) 293-8337

Chesapeake
401 Albemarle Dr
23320
(757) 382-6159

Danville
427 Patton St
24541
(804) 799-6510

Hampton
1928 W Pembroke Ave
23669
(757) 926-2540

Harrisonburg
181 S Liberty St
22801
(540) 434-2545

Leesburg
65 Plaza St
Loudoun County 20176
(703) 771-4500

Lexington
258 Greenhouse Rd
24450
(540) 463-7328

Lynchburg
823 Clay St
24505
(804) 847-1301

Manassas
9518 Fairview Ave
20110
(703) 257-8000

Newport News
224 26th St
23607
(757) 926-8759

Norfolk
811 W City Hall Ave
23510
(757) 664-4955

Petersburg
8 Courthouse Ave
23803
(804) 733-2369

Portsmouth
701 Crawford St
23704
(757) 393-8210

Prince William
1 Cnty Complex Ct
Prince William County 22192
(703) 792-6650

Richmond
1701 Fairfield Way
23223
(804) 646-6600

Roanoke
340 W Campbell Ave
24016
(540) 853-2941

Salem
2 E Calhoun St
24153
(540) 387-0189

Staunton
PO Box 64
24402
(540) 332-3880

Suffolk
150 N Main St
23434
(757) 923-2200

Virginia Beach
2501 James Madison Blvd
23456
(757) 427-4955

Williamsburg
349-51 Court St
23185
(757) 229-2832

WASHINGTON

Auburn
101 N Division
King County 98001
(253) 931-3080

Bellevue
11511 Main St
King County 98004
(425) 452-6917

Bellingham
505 Grand Ave
Whatcom County 98225
(360) 676-6920

Bothell
18916 N Creek Pkwy #103
King County 98011
(425) 486-1254

Bremerton
239 4th St
Kitsap County 98337
(360) 478-5224

Des Moines
21900 11th Ave S
King County 98198
(206) 878-3301

Edmonds
250 5th Ave N
Snohomish County 98020
(425) 771-0200

Everett
3002 Wetmore Ave
Snohomish County 98201
(425) 257-8402

Federal Way
34008 9th Ave S
King County 98003
(253) 661-4600

Kennewick
741 S Dayton St
Benton County 99336
(509) 585-4221

Kent
220 4th Ave S
King County 98032
(253) 856-5800

Kirkland
123 5th Ave
King County 98033
(425) 828-1183

Lacey
420 College St SE
Thurston County 98503
(360) 459-4333

Lakewood
5504 112th St SW
Pierce County 98499
(253) 798-4200

Lynnwood
19321 44th Ave W
Snohomish County 98036
(425) 774-6949

Olympia
900 Plum St SE
Thurston County 98501
(360) 753-8300

Pasco
525 N 3rd Ave
Franklin County 99301
(509) 545-3481

Puyallup
311 W Pioneer Ave
Pierce County 98371
(253) 841-5415

Redmond
8701 160th Ave NE
King County 98073
(425) 556-2500

Renton
1055 S Grady Way
King County 98055
(425) 235-2600

Richland
505 Swift Blvd
Benton County 99352
(509) 942-7360

Seattle
610 Third Ave Rm 1001
King County 98104
(206) 684-5577

Spokane
1100 W Mallon Ave
Spokane County 99260
(509) 625-4050

Tacoma
930 Tacoma Ave S Rm 340
Pierce County 98402
(253) 591-5905

Vancouver
300 W 13th St
Clark County 98660
(360) 696-8292

Walla Walla
15 N Third
Walla Walla County 99362
(509) 527-4434

Yakima
200 S 3rd St
Yakima County 98901
(509) 575-6200

WEST VIRGINIA

Charleston
501 Virginia St E
Kanawha County 25301
(304) 348-6460

Huntington
675 10th St
Cabell County 25701
(304) 696-5510

Morgantown
300 Spruce St
Monongalia County 26505
(304) 284-7522

Parkersburg
1 Government Sq
Wood County 26102
(304) 424-8444

Wheeling
1500 Chapline St
Ohio County 26003
(304) 234-3637

WISCONSIN

Appleton
222 S Walnut St
Outagamie County 54911
(920) 832-5500

Beloit
100 State St
Rock County 53511
(608) 364-6807

Brookfield
2100 N Calhoun Rd
Waukesha County 53005
(262) 782-6200

Eau Claire
740 Second Ave
Eau Claire County 54702
(715) 839-4972

Fond Du Lac
180 S Macy St
Fond Du Lac County 54935
(920) 929-3206

Franklin
9229 W Loomis Rd
Milwaukee County 53132
(414) 425-2522

Green Bay
307 S Adams St
Brown County 54301
(920) 448-3200

Greenfield
5300 W Layton Ave
Milwaukee County 53220
(414) 761-5300

Janesville
18 N Jackson St
Rock County 53545
(608) 757-2544

La Crosse
400 L Crosse St
La Crosse County 54601
(608) 789-7200

Madison
211 S Carroll St
Dane County 53703
(608) 266-4275

Manitowoc
910 Jay St
Manitowoc County 54220
(920) 686-6500

Menomonee Falls
W156 N8480 Pilgrim Rd
Waukesha County 53051
(262) 251-6063

Milwaukee
749 W State St
Milwaukee County 53201
(414) 933-4444

New Berlin
16300 W National Ave
Waukesha County 53151
(262) 782-6640

Oak Creek
7625 S Howell Ave
Milwaukee County 53154
(414) 762-8200

Oshkosh
420 Jackson St
Winnebago County 54901
(920) 236-5700

Sheboygan
828 Center Ave
Sheboygan County 53081
(920) 459-3333

Superior
1409 Hammond Ave
Douglas County 54880
(715) 394-0234

Waukesha
1901 Delafield St
Waukesha County 53188
(262) 524-3761

Wausau
515 Grand Ave
Marathon County 54403
(715) 849-7798

Wauwatosa
1700 N 116th St
Milwaukee County 53226
(414) 471-8430

West Allis
11301 W Lincoln Ave
Milwaukee County 53227
(414) 302-8000

West Bend
1115 S Main St
Washington County 53095
(262) 335-5001

WYOMING

Casper
201 N David St
Natrona County 82601
(307) 235-8225

Cheyenne
2020 Capitol Ave
Laramie County 82001
(307) 637-6521

Laramie
620 Plaza Ct
Albany County 82070
(307) 721-2526

STATE

STATE POLICE-HIGHWAY PATROLS

ALABAMA

James H Alexander
Director
PO Box 1511
Montgomery 36102
(334) 242-4394

ALASKA

Col Glenn G Godfrey
Director
5700 E Tudor Rd
Anchorage 99507
(907) 269-5511

ARIZONA

Dennis A Garrett
Director
PO Box 6638
Phoenix 85005
(602) 223-2000

ARKANSAS

Col Thomas A Mars
Director
1 State Police Plz Dr
Little Rock 72209
(501) 618-8200

CALIFORNIA

D O Helmick
Commissioner
PO Box 942898
Sacramento 94298
(916) 657-7152

COLORADO

Col Lonnie J Westphal
Chief
700 Kipling St Ste 3000
Denver 80215
(303) 239-4403

CONNECTICUT

Dr Henry C Lee
Commissioner
1111 Country Club Rd
Middletown 06457
(860) 685-8000

DELAWARE

Col Gerald R Pepper
Superintendent
1441 N DuPont Hwy
Dover 19901
(302) 739-5911

FLORIDA

Col Charles C Hall
Director
Neil Kirkman Bldg
Tallahassee 32399
(850) 488-4885

GEORGIA

Col Robert E Hightower
Commissioner
PO Box 1456
Atlanta 30372
(404) 624-7710

HAWAII

Daniel Fernandez
Administrator
1111 Alakea St 1st Fl
Honolulu 96813
(808) 538-5656

IDAHO

Col Edwin D Strickfaden
Director
700 S Strafford Dr
Meridian 83642
(208) 884-7003

ILLINOIS

Sam W Nolen
Director
PO Box 19461
Springfield 62794
(217) 782-7263

INDIANA

Melvin J Carraway
Superintendent
100 N Senate Ave
Indianapolis 46204
(317) 232-8241

IOWA

Col Robert O Garrison
Chief
Wallace State Office Bldg
Des Moines 50319
(515) 284-5824

KANSAS

Col Don Brownlee
Superintendent
122 SW 7th St
Topeka 66603
(785) 296-6800

KENTUCKY

Robert F Stephens
Acting Commissioner
919 Versailles Rd
Frankfort 40601
(502) 695-6300

LOUISIANA

Col R W (Rutt) Whittington
Superintendent
PO Box 66614
Baton Rouge 70896
(225) 925-6117

MAINE

Col Michael R Sperry
Chief
36 Hospital St 42 SHS
Augusta 04333
(207) 624-7068

MARYLAND

Col David B Mitchell
Superintendent
1201 Reistertown Rd
Pikesville 21208
(410) 486-3101

MASSACHUSETTS

Col John DiFava
Acting Superintendent
470 Worcester Rd
Framingham 01702
(508) 820-2300

MICHIGAN

Col Michael Robinson
Director
714 S Harrison Rd
East Lansing 48823
(517) 332-2521

MINNESOTA

Col Anne Beers
Chief
444 Cedar St Ste 130
St Paul 55101
(651) 297-3935

MISSISSIPPI

The Hon Ron Ford
Interim Commissioner
PO Box 958
Jackson 39205
(601) 987-1490

MISSOURI

Col W L Wilhoit
Superintendent
PO Box 568
Jefferson City 65102
(573) 751-3313

MONTANA

Col Bert J Obert
Chief
2550 Prospect Ave
Helena 59620
(406) 444-3780

NEBRASKA

Col Tom Nesbitt
Superintendent
1600 Nebraska Hwy 2
Lincoln 68502
(402) 471-4545

NEVADA

Col Michael E Hood
Chief
555 Wright Way
Carson City 89711
(775) 684-4867

NEW HAMPSHIRE

Col Gary M Sloper
Director
10 Hazen Dr
Concord 03305
(603) 271-3636

NEW JERSEY

Col Carson J Dunbar
Superintendent
PO Box 7068
West Trenton 08628
(609) 882-2000

NEW MEXICO

Nicholas Bakas
Cabinet Secretary
PO Box 1628
Santa Fe 87504
(505) 827-3370

NEW YORK

James W McMahon
Superintendent
1220 Washington Ave Bldg 22
Albany 12226
(518) 457-6721

NORTH CAROLINA

Col Richard W Holden
Commander
4702 Mail Service Ctr
Raleigh 27699
(919) 733-7952

NORTH DAKOTA

Col James M Hughes
Superintendent
600 E Boulevard Ave Dept 504
Bismarck 58505
(701) 328-2455

OHIO

Col Kenneth B Marshall
Superintendent
1970 W Broad St
Columbus 43218
(614) 466-2990

OKLAHOMA

Bob A Ricks
Commissioner
PO Box 11415
Oklahoma City 73136
(405) 425-2001

OREGON

R C Ruecker
Superintendent
400 Public Svc Bldg
Salem 97310
(503) 378-3720

PENNSYLVANIA

Col Paul J Evanko
Commissioner
1800 Elmerton Ave
Harrisburg 17110
(717) 772-6924

RHODE ISLAND

Col Edmond S Culhane Jr
Superintendent
311 Danielson Pike
North Scituate 02857
(401) 444-1000

SOUTH CAROLINA

Col R L Mobley
Deputy Director
Law Enfcmnt Division
5400 Broad River Rd
Columbia 29212
(803) 896-7920

SOUTH DAKOTA

Col Tom Dravland
Superintendent
500 E Capitol Ave
Pierre 57501
(605) 773-3105

TENNESSEE

Michael C Greene
Commissioner
1150 Foster Ave
Nashville 37249
(615) 251-5166

TEXAS

Col Thomas Davis
Director
PO Box 4087
Austin 78773
(512) 424-2000

UTAH

Col Richard A Greenwood
Superintendent
4501 S 2700 W Box 141100
Salt Lake City 84114
(801) 965-4062

VERMONT

Col A James Walton Jr
Commissioner
103 S Main St Waterbury State Complex
Waterbury 05671
(802) 244-8718

VIRGINIA

Lt W Gerald Massengill
Acting Superintendent
PO Box 27472
Richmond 23261
(804) 674-2000

WASHINGTON

Annette M Sandberg
Chief
11th & Columbia
Olympia 98504
(360) 753-6540

WEST VIRGINIA

Col Gary L Edgell
Superintendent
725 Jefferson Rd
S Charleston 25309
(304) 746-2111

WISCONSIN

David L Schumacher
Superintendent
4802 Sheboygan Ave Hill Farms State Transp Bldg
Madison 53707
(608) 266-3908

WYOMING

Col John Cox
Administrator/Patrol Division
5300 Bishop Blvd
Cheyenne 82003
(307) 777-4301[3]

OTHER STATE AGENCIES

ABC Enforcement
Adult Institutions Division of Operations
Alcohol Beverage Control Division
Army National Guard Headquarters
Attorney General
Bureau of Services
Central Bureau of Parole
Conservation Offices
Department of Corrections
Department of Environmental Protection and Energy
Department of Human Services
Department of Military and Veterans Affairs
Division of Civil Rights
Division of Consumer Affairs
Division of Criminal Justice
Division of Gaming Enforcement
Forest Fire Services
Insurance Fraud Division
Marine Services Unit
Office of Aviation
Parkway Administration
Poison Information and Education
Police Training Commission
Racing Commission
State Board of Medical Examiners
State House
State Police Communications Bureau
State Police Explosive Disposal
State Police Laboratories
State Police Training Bureau
State Ranger
Treasury Taxation Office
Turnpike Administration
Youth Correctional Institutions Division of Operations

FEDERAL AND SPECIAL PROGRAMS

Air Force Special Investigation
Alcohol, Tobacco and Firearms
Bridge Commission
College and University Police
Defense Criminal Investigation Service
Defense Investigation Service

Department of Commerce
Department of Defense
Department of Health and Human Services
Department of the Navy
Drug Enforcement Administration
EMS Helicopter Response Program
Explosive Ordinance Detachments
Federal Bureau of Investigation
General Services Administration
Internal Revenue Criminal Investigation Division
Internal Revenue Inspection Service
Military Police
National Insurance Crime Bureau
Office of Emergency Medical Services (Mobile Intensive Care Units)
Port Authority
Railroad Police
U.S. Attorney's Office
U.S. Coast Guard
U.S. Customs Service
U.S. Department of Agriculture
U.S. Department of the Interior
U.S. Department of Labor
U.S. Department of State
U.S. Department of Transportation
U.S. District Court Pretrial Service
U.S. District Court Probation
U.S. Environmental Protection Agency
U.S. Homeland Security/Citizenship and Immigration Services
U.S. Marshals Service
U.S. Nuclear Regulatory Commission
U.S. Postal Inspection Services
U.S. Secret Service
U.S. Securities and Exchange Commission
U.S. Department of Veterans Affairs
Waterfront Commission

CHAPTER SIX

CORRECTIONAL INTERNSHIPS

CHAPTER SIX: CORRECTIONAL INTERNSHIPS

INTRODUCTION

The corrections portion of the criminal justice system serves several purposes:

1. To punish offenders
2. To rehabilitate the wrongdoer
3. To deter potential offenders
4. To provide a safe environment for the public

CHAPTER OUTLINE

This chapter will cover the subsequent topics:

1. Correctional Statistics
2. Conditions and Employment
3. Diversity Among Corrections Workers
4. Levels of Correctional Employment
5. Privatization of Corrections
6. Special Programs
7. Parole Programs
8. State Corrections Departments

9. Federal and Special Corrections

CORRECTIONAL STATISTICS

The national crime rate has dropped since the early nineties; however, the number of persons in correctional systems continues to increase. The increase can be examined in the federal, state, and local levels. The Bureau of Justice Statistics reveals the following:

1. The national incarceration rate has more than doubled between 1986 and 1998.
2. The U.S. prisons and jails held a record 1.8 million inmates in 1998. This represents a 4.4% increase (or 76,700 inmates) over 1997.
3. The total sentenced population in federal correctional facilities has more than tripled between 1986 and 1998.
4. The number of women in prison has more than tripled between 1985 and 1997, rising to 138,000.
5. the total number of juveniles held in public correctional facilities rose 47% between 1983 and 1995.[4]

CONDITIONS AND EMPLOYMENT

The trends translate into significant employment growth for correctional professionals of all types—from correctional officers to parole and probation officers to social workers. The Bureau of Labor Statistics ranks corrections officers in the top twenty (25) of all occupations for projected numerical job growth between 1996 and 2006. The Bureau predicts that over 100,000 new corrections officers positions will be created during the ten-year span.[5]

The employment opportunities for correctional officers are expected to be favorable through the year 2006. The need to replace correctional officers who transfer to other occupations or leave the labor force, coupled with rising employment demand, will generate many thousands of job openings each year.

Employment of correctional officers is expected to increase faster than the average for all occupations throughout the year 2006 as additional officers are hired to supervise and control a growing inmate population.

Finally, layoffs of correctional officers are rare because security must be maintained in correctional institutions at all times.

DIVERSITY AMONG CORRECTIONS WORKERS

The Bureau of Justice Statistics reveals that the 347,320 individuals employed in correctional facilities in 1995, 6.3% or (220,982 individuals), worked in custody and securities.

The male/female distribution statistics for corrections employees are comparable to those in law enforcement. In 1995, females made up 28.9% of the employees in correctional facilities. The federal correctional facilities reveal 22.1% of their workers were females who served in the capacity of custody/security personnel.

The African-Americans comprise 29.2% of the correctional institution officers employed nationwide. The Bureau of Labor Statistics states that the corrections professions ranks fourth among occupations held by African-Americans.[6]

LEVELS OF CORRECTIONAL EMPLOYMENT

Like law enforcement and courts, corrections is divided into an adult and a juvenile system.

The levels of corrections officers are divided into:

1. State Department of Corrections
2. Federal Department of Corrections
3. County Department of Corrections

The basic information regarding the six common correctional positions will be discussed subsequently.

CORRECTIONAL COUNSELOR

Description

Evaluate prison inmates' cases, examin counseling needs for rehabilitation; develop training and treatment programs (including substance abuse); and prepare case reports for the U.S. Parole Commission.

Requirements

US citizen
Drug screening
Not to exceed 37 years old
Bachelor's degree and graduate education in behavioral science
Counseling abilities
Written and verbal communication skills

Contact Information

Contact your state department of corrections for state employer opportunities. For federal opportunities contact: The Federal Bureau of Prisons (www.bop.gov).

Mid-Atlantic Regional Office: (303) 317-3211
North Central Regional Office: (913) 551-1193)
Northeast Regional Office: (800) 787-2749
South Central Region: (800) 726-4473
Southeast Region: (888) 789-1022)
Western Region: (925) 803-4700

National Institute of Corrections
320 First Street NW
Washington, DC 20534
(800) 995-6423
www.nicic.org/inst/

American Correctional Association
4380 Forbes Boulevard
Lanham, MD 20706
(800) 222-5646

CORRECTIONAL OFFICER

Description

Corrections officers are responsible for monitoring arrestees awaiting trial and those who have been imprisoned. The duties include monitoring activities of prisoners, enforcing rules and maintaining order, and inspecting correctional facilities and prisoners for illegal substances. There were 320,000 correctional officers employed in 1996 across the nation.

Requirements

Eighteen years of age
U.S. citizen
Possess a high school diploma or equivalent
No prior felony conviction

The Federal Bureau of Prisons requires one of the following in order to obtain a GS-5 level:

Bachelor's degree
Three years work experience
Undergraduate experience and work experience that equals that of 3 years

Contact Information

Contact your state department of corrections for state opportunities. Federal opportunities can be pursued by contacting the Federal Bureau of Prisons. www.bop.gov. Also see prior section for regions and contact information for regional offices.

PAROLE OFFICER

Description

A parole officer is responsible for the legal custody of an offender, after they are released from incarceration, and making sure they abide by the conditions of their release to parole. Parole officers provide counseling and support to help parolees reenter society. Their duties include the educating of the offender on parole guidelines, monitoring parolee behavior by direct contact or indirectly by utilizing modern technology—electronic reporting, phone calls and e-mail.

Requirements

Bachelor's degree or prior experience in parole or probation
US citizen
Valid driver's license
No prior felony convictions
Written and oral examination
Background investigation
Drug screening

Contact Information

American Probation and Parole Association
The Council of State Government:
PO Box 11910
Lexington, KY   40579
(606) 244-8204
www.appa-net.org

US Office of Personnel Management
1900 E. Street NW
Washington, DC   20415
(202) 606-1800
www. Opm-gov

Job Hotline: (912) 757-3000

PROBATION OFFICER

Description

The probation officer is responsible for counseling and rehabilitating offenders without the use of incarceration. Probation officers evaluate crimes and offenders, make recommendations to the court and facilitate a probation agreement between the federal, state or local courts.

Requirements

Bachelor's degree and/or experience in probation
US citizen
Driver's license
Drug screening
Medical and psychological screening

Contact Information

American Probation and Parole Association
Parole Association
The Council of State Governments
PO Box 11910
Lexington, KY   40579
(606) 244-8204
www.appa -net.org

SOCIAL WORKER

Description

The social worker helps people address and cope with their personal, social and community problems, which can include substance abuse, chronic disease, employment stress and family dysfunction. Social workers are typically specialized in their capacity such as clinical/mental, policy and planning, hospital, juvenile, criminal justice (pretrial services) and occupational work.

Requirements

Bachelor's degree in social work from a school accredited by the
  Council on Social Work Education
US citizen

Contact Information

National Association of Social Workers
750 First Street NE Suite 700
Washington, DC   20002
(202) 408-8600
www.naswdc.org

American Association of State Social Work Boards
400 South Ridge Parkway
Suite B
Culpepper, VA   22701
(800) 225-6880
www.aasswb.org

WARDEN

The warden is responsible for the administrative and organizational control of a designated prison through the supervision, security and facilitation of training inmates. The duties may extend outside the institution, and within the institution include enforcing rules and regulations for safety, health, and protection of both inmates and the community.

Requirements

Pass a background investigation
Interview
US citizen
Must not exceed thirty-five years of age

Contact Information

The federal employment opportunities mandate that you contact the Federal Bureau of Prisons (www.bop.gov).

PRIVATIZATION OF CORRECTIONS

There has been an increase of the privatization of correctional facilities and services. This trend will not affect the overall availability of corrections jobs, but it may impact the working conditions at individual facilities or facilities in certain states or regions.

The number of privately owned and operated correctional facilities has gone from 16,000 in 1978 to 150,000 in the present day. The states that indicate the greatest number of privately owned and operated prisons are Texas and California. The other states that utilize private operators are:

1. Connecticut
2. Mississippi
3. New Mexico
4. Idaho
5. Oklahoma
6. Utah
7. Wisconsin
8. Colorado
9. Montana[7]

SPECIAL PROGRAMS

JUVENILE CORRECTIONS AND DRUG COURTS

The juvenile corrections and drug courts are two sub-fields of the corrections industry that have undergone significant expansion in recent years, leading to new internship opportunities.

The US Office of Juvenile Justice and Delinquency Prevention reflects an increase in the demand for juvenile corrections professionals. The total number of juveniles held in public correctional facilities has increased by fifty percent since the 1980's. Also juvenile arrests have increased by at least fifty percent since the mid 1980's.[8]

The drug courts represent a new kind of opportunity for the intern. There are approximately five hundred (500) drug courts that have been implemented to address the drug problems and to combat substance abuse and related crimes.[9]

PAROLE PROGRAMS

PAROLE AND PROBATION

The parole and probation programs have come under extensive attacks from the public and special interest groups who believe said programs put the general public at risk. The programs have been challenged since they do not effectively rehabilitate convicted criminals. There seems to be an increase of convicted criminals on probation and parole. The numbers of both have exceeded the four (4) million mark.[10]

Therefore, the Bureau of Labor Statistics estimates an above average growth in the number of probation and parole officer positions between 1996 and 2008.[11]

STATE CORRECTIONS DEPARTMENTS

ALABAMA

DEPARTMENT OF CORRECTIONS
PO Box 301501, 101 S Union St, Montgomery 36130-1501
(334) 353-3870
http://www.agencies.state.al.us/doc/

DEPARTMENT OF YOUTH SERVICES
PO Box 66, Mt. Meigs 36057-0066
(334) 215-3800

ALASKA

DEPARTMENT OF CORRECTIONS
Office of the Commissioner-Juneau
240 Main St, Ste 700, Juneau 99801
(907) 465-4652
http://www.correct.state.ak.us

DIVISION OF INSTITUTIONS
4500 Diplomacy Dr, Ste 207, Anchorage 99508-5918
(907) 269-7409

DIVISION OF COMMUNITY CORRECTIONS
4500 Diplomacy Dr, Ste 207, Anchorage 99508-5918
(907) 269-7370

DIVISION OF FAMILY AND YOUTH SERVICES
PO Box 110635, Juneau 99811-0630
(907) 465-2212
http://www.has.state.ak.us/dfys

ARIZONA

DEPARTMENT OF CORRECTIONS
1601 W Jefferson, Phoenix 85007
(602) 542-5497
http://www.state.az.us/doc

DEPARTMENT OF JUVENILE CORRECTIONS
1624 W Adams, Phoenix 85007
(602) 542-3987
http://www.juvenile.state.az.us

ARKANSAS

DEPARTMENT OF CORRECTIONS
PO Box 8707, Pine Bluff 71611-8707
(870) 267-6200

DEPARTMENT OF COMMUNITY PUNISHMENT
105 West Capitol, 2nd Floor, Two Union National Plaza, Little Rock 72201
(501) 682-9510

DEPARTMENT OF HUMAN SERVICES
Donaghey Plaza W, PO Box 1437, Slot 344, Little Rock 72203-1437

CALIFORNIA

YOUTH AND ADULT CORRECTIONAL AGENCY
1100 11th St, Ste 4000, Sacramento 95814
(916) 323-6001

DEPARTMENT OF CORRECTIONS
1515 S St, PO Box 942883, Sacramento 94283-0001
(916) 445-7688
http://www.cdc.state.ca.us

PAROLE AND COMMUNITY SERVICES DIVISION
1515 S St, Rm 212N, Sacramento 95814
(916) 323-0576

DEPARTMENT OF THE YOUTH AUTHORITY
4241 Williamsbourgh Dr, Sacramento 95823
(916) 262-1467
http://www.cya.ca.gov

PAROLE SERVICES AND COMMUNITY CORRECTIONS
(916) 262-1363

COLORADO

DEPARTMENT OF CORRECTIONS
2862 S Circle Dr, Ste 400, Colorado Springs 80906-4195
(719) 579-9580
http://www.state.co.us/gov-dir/doc-dir

DIVISION OF ADULT PAROLE SUPERVISION
10403 W Colfax, Ste 7000, Lakewood 80215
(303) 238-5967

DIVISION OF COMMUNITY CORRECTIONS
12157 W Cedar Drive, Lakewood 80228
(303) 985-9805

DEPARTMENT OF HUMAN SERVICES
1575 Sherman St, 8th Fl, Denver 80203-1714
(303) 866-5096

DIVISION OF YOUTH CORRECTIONS
4255 S Knox Ct, Denver 80236-3195
(303) 866-7345
http://www.cdns.state.co.us/dyc/home.html

CONNECTICUT

DEPARTMENT OF CORRECTIONS
24 Wolcott Hill Rd, Wethersfield 06109-1152
(860) 692-7482
http://www.state.ct.us/doc

OFFICE OF ADULT PROBATION
2275 Silas Deane Hwy, Rocky Hill 06067
(860) 529-1316

DEPARTMENT OF CHILDREN AND FAMILIES
505 Hudson St, Hartford 06106
(860) 550-6300
http://www.state.ct.us/dcf

DELAWARE

DEPARTMENT OF CORRECTIONS
245 McKee Rd, Dover 19904
(302) 739-5601
http://www.state.de.us/correct/ddoc/default.htm

BUREAU OF COMMUNITY CORRECTIONS
(302) 739-5601

DEPARTMENT OF SERVICES FOR CHILDREN, YOUTH, AND THEIR FAMILIES
1825 Faukland Rd, Wilmington 19805
(302) 633-2500

DISTRICT OF COLUMBIA

DEPARTMENT OF CORRECTIONS
1923 Vermont Ave NW, Washington 20001
(202) 673-7316

SOCIAL SERVICES DIVISION
DC Superior Court, 409 E St NW, Washington 20001
(202) 508-1800

DEPARTMENT OF HUMAN SERVICES
609 H St NE, Washington 20002
(202) 698-4600

FLORIDA

DEPARTMENT OF CORRECTIONS
2601 Blair Stone Rd, Tallahassee 32399-2500
(850) 488-7480
www.dc.state.fl.us

DEPARTMENT OF JUVENILE JUSTICE
2737 Centerview Dr, Knight Bldg, Tallahassee 32399-3100
(850) 921-0904
http://www.djj.state.fl.us

GEORGIA

DEPARTMENT OF CORRECTIONS
Floyd Bldg, Twin Towers E, Ste 866, 2 Martin Luther King Jr Dr SE, Atlanta 30334
(404) 656-6002
gdccommish@dcor.state.ga.us

DEPARTMENT OF JUVENILE JUSTICE
2 Peachtree St, 5th Fl, Atlanta 30303
(404) 657-2401
http://www.doas.state.ga.us/Dpeartments/DJJ

HAWAII

DEPARTMENT OF PUBLIC SAFETY (CORRECTIONS)
919 Ala Moana Blvd, Honolulu 96814
(808) 587-1350
http://www.state.hi.us/icsd/psd/psd.html

COMMUNITY CORRECTIONAL CENTERS DIVISION
Hawaii Community Correctional Center, 60 Punahele St, Hilo 96720
(808) 933-0428

IDAHO

DEPARTMENT OF CORRECTIONS
1299 N Orchard St, Ste 110, Boise 83706
(208) 658-2000
http://www.corr.state.id.us

DEPARTMENT OF JUVENILE CORRECTIONS
400 N 10th, 2nd Fl, PO Box 83720, Boise 83720-0285
(208) 334-5102
http://www.djc.state.id.us

ILLINOIS

DEPARTMENT OF CORRECTIONS
1301 Concordia Ct, PO Box 19277, Springfield 62794-9277
(217) 522-2666
http://www.idoc.state.il.us

COMMUNITY SERVICES DIVISION
1301 Concordia Ct, PO Box 19277, Springfield 62794-9277
(217) 522-2666

DEPARTMENT OF CORRECTIONS
2700 S California Ave, Chicago 60608
(773) 869-2859

ADULT PROBATION DEPARTMENT
69 W Washington, Ste 2000, Chicago 60602
(312) 603-0258

INDIANA

DEPARTMENT OF CORRECTIONS
Indiana Government Center South, 302 W Washington St, Rm E334, Indianapolis 46204-2278
(317) 232-5715
http://www.state.in.us/indcorrection

DIVISION OF JUVENILE SERVICES
(317) 232-1746
http://www.state.in.us/fssa/HTML/PROGRAMS/za.html

IOWA

DEPARTMENT OF CORRECTIONS
420 Keo Way, Des Moines 50309
(515) 242-5703
http://www.sos.state.ia.us/register/r4/r4corre2.htm

DEPARTMENT OF HUMAN SERVICES
Hoover State Office Bldg, Des Moines 50319
(515) 281-5452

KANSAS

DEPARTMENT OF CORRECTIONS
Landon State Office Bldg, 4th Fl, 900 SW Jackson, Topeka 66612-1284
(785) 296-3317
http://www.ink.org/public/kdoc

DIVISION OF COMMUNITY AND FIELD SERVICES
(785) 296-4520

JUVENILE JUSTICE AUTHORITY
Jayhawk Walk, 714 SW Jackson, Ste 300, Topeka 66603
(785) 296-4213
http://www.ink.org/public/kjja

KENTUCKY

DEPARTMENT OF CORRECTIONS
PO Box 2400, Frankfort 40601-2400
(502) 564-4726

ADULT INSTITUTIONS
(502) 564-2220

COMMUNITY SERVICES AND LOCAL FACILITIES
(502) 564-7023

DEPARTMENT OF JUVENILE JUSTICE
1025 Capital Center Dr, 3rd Fl, Frankfort 40601
(502) 573-2738
http://www.jus.state.ky.us/djj

LOUISIANA

CORRECTIONS SERVICES
PO Box 94304, Capitol Station, Baton Rouge 70804-9304
(225) 342-5723

DIVISION OF PROBATION AND PAROLE
504 Mayflower St, Baton Rouge 70802
(225) 342-6609

DIVISION OF YOUTH SERVICES-PROBATION SERVICES
Division of Youth Services, PO Box 94304, Baton Rouge 70804-9304
(225) 342-2642

MAINE

DEPARTMENT OF CORRECTIONS
State House Station 111, Augusta 04333
(207) 287-4360
http://www.state.me.us/corrections/homepage

DIVISION OF PROBATION AND PAROLE
State House Station 111, Augusta 04333
(207) 287-4384

MARYLAND

DEPARTMENT OF PUBLIC SAFETY AND CORRECTIONAL SERVICES
Ste 1000, 300 E Joppa Rd, Towson 21286-3020
(410) 339-5000
http://www.dpscs.state.md.us/doc

DIVISION OF CORRECTIONS
6776 Reisterstown Rd, Ste 310, Baltimore 21215-2342
(410) 285-3300

DIVISION OF PAROLE AND PROBATION
6776 Reisterstown Rd, Ste 305, Baltimore 21215-2349
(410) 764-4274

DEPARTMENT OF JUVENILE JUSTICE
One Center Plaza, 120 W Fayette St, Baltimore 21201
(410) 230-3100
http://www.djj.state.md.us

MASSACHUSETTS

EXECUTIVE OFFICE OF PUBLIC SAFETY
John W. McCormick State Office Bldg, 1 Ashburton Pl, Rm 2133, 21st Fl, Boston 02108
(617) 727-7775

DEPARTMENT OF CORRECTIONS
Central Headquarters, 50 Maple St, Ste 3, Milford 01757
(508) 422-3348
http://www.magnet.state.ma.us/doc/

OFFICE OF THE COMMISSIONER OF PROBATION
One Ashburton Pl, Rm 405, Boston 02108
(617) 727-5300

EXECUTIVE OFFICE OF HEALTH AND HUMAN SERVICES
One Ashburton Pl, Rm 1109, Boston 02108
(617) 727-7600

MICHIGAN

DEPARTMENT OF CORRECTIONS
Grandview Plaza Bldg, PO Box 30003, Lansing 48909
(517) 373-0720

OFFICE OF COMMUNITY CORRECTIONS
PO Box 30003, Lansing 48909
(517) 373-0415

CHILD AND FAMILY SERVICES ADMINISTRATION
(517) 335-6158

MINNESOTA

DEPARTMENT OF CORRECTIONS
1450 Energy Park Dr, Ste 200, St. Paul 55108-5219
(651) 642-0282
http://www.corr.state.mn.us

PROBATION, PAROLE, AND SUPERVISED RELEASE OFFICES
1450 Energy Park Dr, Ste 200, St. Paul 55108-5219
(651) 603-0181

MISSISSIPPI

DEPARTMENT OF CORRECTIONS
723 N President St, Jackson 39202-3097
(601) 359-5600
http://www.mdoc.state.ms.us/mdoc/Default/htm

COMMUNITY SERVICES DIVISION
723 N President St, Jackson 39202
(601) 359-5600

DIVISION OF YOUTH SERVICES
PO Box 352, Jackson 39205
(601) 359-4972
http://www.state.ms.us/dys.html

COMMUNITY SERVICES DIVISION
(601) 359-4955

MISSOURI

DEPARTMENT OF CORRECTIONS
PO Box 236, 2729 Plaza Dr, Jefferson City 65102-0236
(573) 751-2389
http://www.corrections.state.mo.us

DEPARTMENT OF SOCIAL SERVICES
Broadway Bldg, Jefferson City 65101
(573) 751-4815

DIVISION OF YOUTH SERVICES
PO Box 447, 5th Fl, Broadway Bldg, Jefferson City 65102-0447
(573) 751-3324
http://www.dss.state.mo.us/dys.htm

MONTANA

DEPARTMENT OF CORRECTIONS
1539 11th Ave, PO Box 201301, Helena 59620-1301
(406) 444-3930

JUVENILE CORRECTIONS
Department of Corrections, 1539 11th Ave, Helena 59620-1301
(406) 232-1377

NEBRASKA

DEPARTMENT OF CORRECTIONAL SERVICES
PO Box 94661, Lincoln 68509-4661
(402) 471-2654
http://www.corrections.state.ne.us

HEALTH AND HUMAN SERVICES AGENCY-PROTECTION AND SAFETY
DIVISION
PO Box 95044, Lincoln 68509-5044
(402) 471-8410

NEBRASKA PROBATION SYSTEM
PO Box 98910, Lincoln 68509
(402) 471-4928

NEVADA

DEPARTMENT OF PRISONS
PO Box 7011, Carson City 89702-7011
(775) 887-3216

DIVISION OF PAROLE AND PROBATION
1445 Hot Springs Rd, Ste 104, Carson City 89710
(775) 687-5040

DIVISION OF CHILD AND FAMILY SERVICES
711 E 5th St, Carson City 99710
(775) 684-4429

YOUTH CORRECTIONS
620 Belrose, Ste C, Las Vegas 89107-2234
(702) 486-5095

NEVADA YOUTH PAROLE BUREAU
620 Belrose, Ste C, Las Vegas 89158
(702) 486-5080
http://www.state.nv.us/dcfs/page21.html

NEW HAMPSHIRE

DEPARTMENT OF CORRECTIONS
PO Box 1806, Concord 03302-1806
(603) 271-5600
http://www.state.nh.us

DIVISION OF FIELD SERVICES
105 Pleasant St, 3rd Fl, Box 1806, Concord 03302-1806
(603) 271-5652

DEPARTMENT OF YOUTH DEVELOPMENT SERVICES
1056 N River Rd, Manchester 03104-1998
(603) 625-5471

NEW JERSEY

DEPARTMENT OF CORRECTIONS
PO Box 863, Trenton 08625-0863
(609) 292-9340
http://www.state.nj.us/corrections

JUVENILE JUSTICE COMMISSION
840 Bear Tavern Rd, PO Box 107, Trenton 08625-0107
(609) 530-5200

DEPARTMENT OF LAW AND PUBLIC SAFETY
PO Box 107, Trenton 08625-0107
(609) 530-5200

NEW MEXICO

CORRECTIONS DEPARTMENT
PO Box 27116, Hwy 14, Santa Fe 87502-0116
(505) 827-8709
http://www.state.nm.us/corrections

ADULT PRISONS DIVISION
PO Box 27116, Santa Fe 87502-0116
(505) 827-8638

PROBATION AND PAROLE DIVISION
PO Box 27116, Santa Fe 87502-0116
(505) 827-8830

CHILDREN, YOUTH AND FAMILIES DEPARTMENT
PO Drawer 5160, Santa Fe 87502-5160
(505) 827-7602
http://www.cyfabq.cyfd.state.nm.us

JUVENILE JUSTICE DIVISIOIN
(505) 827-7629

JUVENILE REINTEGRATION CENTERS
300 San Mateo Blvd, Ste 410, Albuquerque 87108
((505) 841-2947

NEW YORK

DEPARTMENT OF CORRECTIONAL SERVICES
1220 Washington Ave, Bldg 2, Albany 12226-2050
(518) 457-8134

DIVISION OF PAROLE
97 Central Ave, Albany 12206
(518) 473-9672

OFFICE OF CHILDREN AND FAMILY SERVICES
52 Washington St, Rensselaer 12144-2735
(518) 473-8437
http://www.dfy.state.ny.us

DIVISON OF PROBATION AND CORRECTIONAL ALTERNATIVES
4 Tower Pl, 3rd Fl, Albany 12203
(518) 485-2395

DEPARTMENT OF CORRECTIONS
60 Hudson St, 6th Fl, New York 10013-4393
(212) 266-1212

DEPARTMENT OF PROBATION
115 Leonard St, New York 10013
(212) 442-4523

NORTH CAROLINA

DEPARTMENT OF CORRECTIONS
214 W Jones St, MSC 4201, Raleigh 27699-4201
(919) 733-4926
http://www.doc.state.nc.us

DIVISION OF PRISONS
831 W Morgan St, MSC 4260, Raleigh 27699-4260
(919) 733-3226

DIVISION OF COMMUNITY CORRECTIONS
2020 Yonkers Rd, 4250 MSC, Raleigh 27669-4250
(919) 716-3100

OFFICE OF JUVENILE JUSTICE
410 S Salisbury St, 1801 MSC, Raleigh 27993-1801
(919) 733-3388

NORTH DAKOTA

DEPARTMENT OF CORRECTIONS AND REHABILITATION
PO Box 1898, Bismarck 58502-1898
(701) 328-6390
http://www.state.nd.us/docr

DIVISION OF ADULT SERVICES
(701) 253-3660

FIELD SERVICES DIVISION, ADULT SERVICES
PO Box 5521, Bismarck 58506-5521
(701) 328-6190

DIVISION OF JUVENILE SERVICES
PO Box 1898, Bismarck 58502-1898
(701) 328-6390

OHIO

DEPARTMENT OF REHABILITATION AND CORRECTION
1050 Freeway Dr N, Columbus 43229
(614) 752-1164
http://www.drc.state.oh.us

ADULT PAROLE AUTHORITY
(614) 752-1254

BUREAU OF COMMUNITY SANCTIONS
(614) 752-1188

BUREAU OF ADULT DETENTION
(614) 752-1065

OFFICE OF VICTIM SERVICES
(614) 728-9947

DEPARTMENT OF YOUTH SERVICES
51 N High St, Columbus 43215-3098
(614) 466-8783
http://www.state.oh.us/dys

OKLAHOMA

DEPARTMENT OF CORRECTIONS
3400 Martin Luther King Ave, Oklahoma City 73136-4298
(405) 425-2500
http://www.doc.state.ok.us

DIVISION OF COMMUNITY SENTENCING
2200 N Classen Blvd, Ste 1900, Oklahoma City 73106-5811
(405) 523-3075

DIVISION OF PROBATION AND PAROLE/COMMUNITY CORRECTIONS
(405) 218-4200

OFFICE OF JUVENILE AFFAIRS
PO Box 268812, 3812 N Santa Fe, Ste 400, Oklahoma City 73126-8812
(405) 530-2800
http://www.state.ok.us/~oja

OREGON

DEPARTMENT OF CORRECTIONS
2575 Center St NE, Salem 97301-6637
(503) 945-0920
http://www.doc.state.or.us

BOARD OF PAROLE AND POST-PRISON SUPERVISION (FT)
2575 Center St NE, Salem 97310-0470
(503) 945-0900

OREGON YOUTH AUTHORITY (OYA)
530 Center St NE, Ste 200, Salem 97301-3765
(503) 373-7205
http://www.oya.state.or.us

PENNSYLVANIA

DEPARTMENT OF CORRECTIONS
Box 598, Camp Hill 17001-0598
(717) 975-4860
http://www.cor.state.pa.us

BUREAU OF COMMUNITY CORRECTIONS
PO Box 598, Camp Hill 17001-0598
(717) 731-7147

BOARD OF PAROBATION AND PAROLE (FT)
1101 S Front St, Ste 5000, Harrisburg 17104-2537
(717) 787-5100

RHODE ISLAND

DEPARTMENT OF CORRECTIONS
40 Howard Ave, Cranston 02920
(401) 462-2611
http://www.doc.state.ri.us

ADULT PROBATION AND PAROLE
J. Joseph Garrahy Judicial Complex, One Dorrance Plaza, Providence 02903
(401) 458-3033

ADULT CORRECTIONAL INSTITUTIONS
(401) 462-5163

DEPARTMENT OF CHILDREN, YOUTH AND FAMILIES
610 Mt. Pleasant Ave, Providence 02908-1935
(401) 222-5307
http://www.state.ri.us/manual/data/queries/stdept_.idc?id=20

SOUTH CAROLINA

DEPARTMENT OF CORRECTIONS
PO Box 21787, 4444 Broad River Rd, Columbia 29221-1787
(803) 896-8555
http://www.state.sc.us/doc

DEPARTMENT OF PROBATION, PAROLE AND PARDON SERVICES
PO Box 50666, 2221 Devine St, Ste 600, Columbia 29250
(803) 734-9220
http://www.state.sc.us/ppp

DEPARTMENT OF JUVENILE JUSTICE
PO Box 21069, 4900 Broad River Rd, Columbia 29221-1069
(803) 896—9791
http://www.state.sc.us/djj

SOUTH DAKOTA

DEPARTMENT OF CORRECTIONS
3200 E Hwy 34, c/o 500 E Capitol Ave, Pierre 57501-5070
(605) 773-3478
http://www.state.sd.us/state/executive/corrections

TENNESSEE

DEPARTMENT OF CORRECTIONS
Rachel Jackson Bldg, 320 Sixth Ave N, 4th Fl, Nashville 37243-0465
(615) 741-1000
http://www.state.tn.us/correction

COMMUNITY CORRECTIONS
(615) 741-3141

DIVISION OF FIELD SERVICES
Ste 1513 Parkway Towers, 404 James Robertson Pkwy, Nashville 37243-0850
(615) 741-3141

DEPARTMENT OF CHILDREN'S SERVICES
Cordell Hull Bldg, 436 6th Ave N, Nashville 37243-1290
(615) 741-9701
http://www.state.tn.us/youth

TEXAS

TEXAS DEPARTMENT OF CRIMINAL JUSTICE
PO Box 99, Spur 59 off Hwy 75 North, Huntsville 77342-0099
(936) 437-2101
http://www.tdcj.state.tx.us

COMMUNITY JUSTICE ASSISTANCE DIVISION (CJAD)
PO Box 12427, Capitol Station, Austin 78701
(512) 305-9300

STATE JAIL DIVISION
PO Box 13084, Austin 78711
(512) 463-7663

INSTITUTIONAL DIVISION
PO Box 99, Huntsville 77342-0099
(936) 437-2169

PAROLE DIVISION
PO Box 13401, Capitol Station, Austin 78711
(512) 406-5401

PROGRAMS AND SERVICES DIVISION
PO Box 99, Huntsville 77342-0099
(936) 437-2180

TEXAS YOUTH COMMISSION
4900 N Lamar, PO Box 4260, Austin 78765
(512) 424-6001
http://www.tyc.state.tx.us/index.html

JUVENILE PROBATION COMMISSION (TJPC)
PO Box 13547, Austin 78711-3547
(512) 424-6682
http://www.tjpc.state.tx.us

UTAH

DEPARTMENT OF CORRECTIONS
6100 S 300 E, Salt Lake City 84107
(801) 265-5500
http://www.cr.ex.state.ut.us

DIVISION OF UTAH CORRECTIONAL INDUSTRIES
PO Box 250. Draper 84020
(801) 576-7700

DIVISION OF ADULT PROBATION AND PAROLE
6100 S 300 E, Salt Lake City 84107
(801) 265-5500

VERMONT

DEPARTMENT OF CORRECTIONS
103 S Main St, Waterbury 05671-1001
(802) 241-2442

DEPARTMENT OF SOCIAL AND REHABILITATION SERVICES
103 S Main St, Osgood Bldg, 3rd Fl, Waterbury 05671-2401
(802) 241-2100

VIRGINIA

DEPARTMENT OF CORRECTIONS
PO Box 26963, 6900 Atmore Dr, Richmond 23261-6963
(804) 674-3119
http://www.cns.state.va.us/doc

DEPARTMENT OF JUVENILE JUSTICE
PO Box 1110, Richmond 23218-1110
(804) 371-0700

WASHINGTON

DEPARTMENT OF CORRECTIONS
PO Box 41100, Olympia 98504-1100
(360) 753-1573
http://www.wa.gov/doc

DEPARTMENT OF CORRECTIONS,
OFFICE OF CORRECTIONAL OPERATIONS
PO Box 41118, Olympia 98504-1118
(360) 753-1502

JUVENILE REHABILITATION ADMINISTRATION
PO Box 45045, Olympia 98504-5045
(360) 902-7804

WEST VIRGINIA

DIVISION OF CORRECTIONS
112 California Ave, Bldg 4, Rm 300, Charleston 25305
(304) 558-2036

DIVISION OF JUVENILE SERVICES
1200 Quarrier St, 2nd Fl, Charleston 25301
(304) 558-6029

WISCONSIN

DEPARTMENT OF CORRECTIONS
PO Box 7925, 149 E Wilson St, Madison 53707-7925
http://www.badger.state.wi.us/agencies/doc

DIVISION OF JUVENILE CORRECTIONS
149 E Wilson St, PO Box 8930, Madison 53708-8930
(608) 267-9507
http://www.badger.state.wi.us/agencies/doc/html/djc.html

WYOMING

DEPARTMENT OF CORRECTIONS
700 W 21st St, Cheyenne 82002-3427
(307) 777-7208
http://www.state.wy.us/~corr/corrections.html

DIVISION OF FIELD SERVICES
700 W 21st St, Cheyenne 82002
(307) 777-7208

DEPARTMENT OF FAMILY SERVICES
Hathaway Bldg, Rm 318, Cheyenne 82002
(307) 777-5994

FEDERAL AND SPECIAL CORRECTIONS

FEDERAL BUREAU OF PRISONS

FEDERAL BUREAU OF PRISONS
320 Fist St NW, HOLC Bldg, Rm 654, Washington, DC 20534
(202) 307-3250
http://www.bop.gov

COMMUNITY CORRECTIONS AND DETENTION DIVISION
(202) 514-8585

CORRECTIONAL PROGRAMS DIVISION
(202) 307-3226

MID-ATLANTIC (ANNAPOLIS JUNCTION, MD)
Junction Business Park, 10010 Junction Dr, Ste 100-N, Annapolis Junction, MD 20701
(301) 317-3100

NORTH CENTRAL (KANSAS CITY)
Gateway Complex Tower II, 8th Fl, 4th & State Ave, Kansas City, KS 66101-2492
(913) 621-3939

NORTHEAST (PHILADELPHIA)
U.S. Customs House, 7th Fl, 2nd & Chestnut Sts, Philadelphia, PA 19106
(215) 521-7300

SOUTH CENTRAL (DALLAS)
4211 Cedar Springs Rd, Ste 300, Dallas, TX 75219
(214) 224-3389

SOUTHEAST (ATLANTA)
3800 North Camp Creek Parkway, SW, Bldg 2000, Atlanta, GA 30331-5099
(678) 686-1200

WESTERN (DUBLIN, CA)
7950 Dublin Blvd, 3rd Fl, Dublin, CA 94568
(925) 803-4700

UNITED STATES PENITENTIARY
3901 Klein Blvd, Lompoc, CA 93436
(805) 735-2771

UNITED STATES PENITENTIARY
PO Box 7500, 5880 State Hwy 67 S, Florence, CO 81226
(719) 784-9454

UNITED STATES PENITENTIARY
601 McDonough Blvd SE, Atlanta, GA 30315-0182
(404) 635-5100

UNITED STATES PENITENTIARY
PO Box 2000, 4500 Prison Rd, Rt 5, Marion, IL 62959
(618) 964-1441

UNITED STATES PENITENTIARY
855 Airbase Rd #1, Pollack, LA 71467
(318) 765-0007

UNITED STATES PENITENTIARY
1300 Metropolitan, Leavenworth, KS 66048
(913) 682-8700

UNITED STATES PENITENTIARY
RD #5, Penn Rd, Lewisburg, PA 17837
(570) 523-1251

UNITED STATES PENITENTIARY
Allenwood, PO Box 3500, White Deer, PA 17887
(570) 547-0963

UNITED STATES PENITENTIARY
Beaumont, PO Box 26035, Beaumont, TX 77720-6035
(409) 727-8188

FEDERAL CORRECTION COMPLEX
Admin Bldg, 846 NE 54th Terr, Coleman, FL 33521-8999
(352) 330-3003

FEDERAL CORRECTION COMPLEX
Low, 846 NE 54th Terr, Coleman, FL 33521-8999
(352) 330-3100

FEDERAL CORRECTION COMPLEX
Medium, 811 NE 54th Terr, Coleman, FL 33521-8997
(352) 330-3200

FEDERAL CORRECTION COMPLEX
Administrative, PO Box 36015, Beaumont, TX 77720-6015
(409) 727-8187

FEDERAL CORRECTION COMPLEX
Low, PO Box 26025, Beaumont, TX 77720-6025
(409) 727-8172

FEDERAL CORRECTION COMPLEX
Medium, PO Box 26045, Beaumont, TX 77720-6045
(409) 727-0101

FEDERAL CORRECTION INSTITUTION
565 E Renfroe Rd, Talladega, AL 35160
(256) 315-4100

FEDERAL CORRECTION INSTITUTION
PO Box 7000, Forrest City, AR 72336
(870) 630-6000

FEDERAL CORRECTION INSTITUTION
37900 N 45th Ave, Dept 1680, Phoenix AZ 85027-7003
(623) 465-9757

FEDERAL CORRECTION INSTITUTION
PO Box 820, Swift Trail Rd, RR 2, Safford, AZ 85548
(520) 428-6600

FEDERAL CORRECTION INSTITUTION
8901 S Wilmot Rd, Tucson, AZ 85706
(520) 574-7100

FEDERAL CORRECTION INSTITUTION
5701 8th St, Camp Parks, Dublin CA 94568
(925) 833-7500

FEDERAL CORRECTION INSTITUTION
3600 Guard Rd, Lompoc, CA 93436
(805) 736-4154

FEDERAL CORRECTION INSTITUTION
1500 Cadette Rd, PO Box 7000, Taft, CA 93268
(661) 763-2510

FEDERAL CORRECTION INSTITUTION
1299 Seaside Ave, Terminal Island, CA 90731-0207
(310) 831-8961

FEDERAL CORRECTION INSTITUTION
15115 Nisqualli Rd, Victorville, CA 92392
(760) 246-2400

FEDERAL CORRECTION INSTITUTION
PO Box 6500, 5880 State Hwy 67 S, Florence CO 81226
(719) 784-9100

FEDERAL CORRECTION INSTITUTION

Englewood, 9595 W Quincy Ave, Littleton, CO 80123
(303) 985-1566

FEDERAL CORRECTION INSTITUTION
Rt 37, Danbury, CT 06811-3099
(203) 743-6471

FEDERAL CORRECTIONAL INSTITUTION
3625 FCI Rd., Marianna, FL 32446
(850) 526-2313

FEDERAL CORRECTIONAL INSTITUTION
15801 SW 137th Ave., Miami, FL 33177
(305) 259-2100

FEDERAL CORRECTIONAL INSTITUTION
501 Capital Circle NE, Tallahassee, FL 32301-3572
(850) 878-2173

FEDERAL CORRECTIONAL INSTITUTION
2600 Hwy 301S, Jesup, GA 31599
(912) 427-0870

FEDERAL CORRECTIONAL INSTITUTION
PO Box 4000, 100 US Rt. 40, Greenville, IL 62246
(618) 664-6200

FEDERAL CORRECTIONAL INSTITUTION
2600 S Second St., PO Box 7000, Pekin, IL 61555-7000
(309) 346-8588

FEDERAL CORRECTIONAL INSTITUTION
PO Box 888, Ashland, KY 41105-0888
(606) 928-6414

FEDERAL CORRECTIONAL INSTITUTION
PO Box 3000, Rt. 8, Fox Hollow Road, Manchester, KY 40962
(606) 598-1900

FEDERAL CORRECTIONAL INSTITUTION
PO Box 5050, E Whatley Rd., Oakdale, LA 71463
(318) 335-4070

FEDERAL CORRECTIONAL INSTITUTION
14601 Burbridge Rd SE, Cumberland, MD 21502-8771
(301) 784-1000

FEDERAL CORRECTIONAL INSTITUTION
 PO Box 9999, East Arkona Rd., Milan, MI 48160
(734) 439-1511

FEDERAL CORRECTIONAL INSTITUTION
Kettle River Rd, Hwy 123, Sandstone, MN 55072
(320) 245-2262

FEDERAL CORRECTIONAL INSTITUTION
 PO Box 1731, 1000 University Dr SW, Waseca, MN 56093
(507) 835-8972

FEDERAL CORRECTIONAL INSTITUTION
PO Box 5050, 2225 Haley Barbour Pkwy, Yazoo City, MS 39194
(601) 751-4800

FEDERAL CORRECTIONAL INSTITUTION
 PO Box 280, Hwy 698, Fairton, NJ 08320
(856) 453-1177

FEDERAL CORRECTIONAL INSTITUTION
PO Box 38, Hartford & Pointville, BLDG 5756, Ft. Dix, NJ 08640
(609) 723-1100

FEDERAL CORRECTIONAL INSTITUTION-La Tuna
PO Box 1000, 8500 Doniphan, Anthony, NM-TX 88021
(915) 886-3422

FEDERAL CORRECTIONAL INSTITUTION
PO Box 600, Two Mile Dr, Otisville, NY 10963-0600
(914) 386-5855

FEDERAL CORRECTIONAL INSTITUTION
PO Box 300, Old Ray Brook Rd, Ray Brook, NY 12977
(518) 891-5400

FEDERAL CORRECTIONAL INSTITUTION LOW
PO Box 999, Old Oxford Hwy 75, Butner, NC 27509
(919) 575-5000

FEDERAL CORRECTIONAL INSTITUTION
 PO Box 1000, Old NC Hwy 75, Butner, NC 27509-1000
(919) 575-4541

FEDERAL CORRECTIONAL INSTITUTION
PO Box 89, 8730 Scroggs Rd, Elkton, OH 44415
(330) 424-7448

FEDERAL CORRECTIONAL INSTITUTION
Hwy 66 W, PO Box 1000, El Reno, OK 73036-1000
(405) 262-4875

FEDERAL CORRECTIONAL INSTITUTION
PO Box 8000, 27072 Ballston Rd, Sheridan, OR 97378-9601
(503) 843-4442

FEDERAL CORRECTIONAL INSTITUTION
McKean, PO Box 5000, Rt. 59, Big Shanty Rd, Bradford, PA 16701
(814) 362-8900

FEDERAL CORRECTIONAL INSTITUTION
PO Box 1000, RR #276, Loretto, PA 15940
(814) 472-4140

FEDERAL CORRECTIONAL INSTITUTION
Schuylkill, PO Box 730, Interstate 81 & 901 W, Minersville, PA 17954
(570) 544-7100

FEDERAL CORRECTIONAL INSTITUTION
Allenwood, Medium, PO Box 2500, Rt 15, White Deer, PA 17887
(570) 547-7950

LOW SECURITY CORRECTIONAL INSTITUTION
Allenwood, PO Box 1500, Rt., 15 White Deer, PA 17887
(570) 547- 1990

FEDERAL CORRECTIONAL INSTITUTION
501 Gary Hill Rd., PO Box 723, Edgefield, SC 29824
(803) 637-1500

FEDERAL CORRECTIONAL INSTITUTION
PO Box 699, 100 Prison Rd., Estill, SC 29918
(803) 625-4607

FEDERAL CORRECTIONAL INSTITUTION
1101 John A. Denie Rd., Memphis, TN 38134-7690
(901) 372-2269

FEDERAL CORRECTIONAL INSTITUTION
PO Box 730, Hwy 95, Bastrop, TX 78602
(512) 321-3903

FEDERAL CORRECTIONAL INSTITUTION
1900 Simler Ave., Big Spring, TX 79720-7799
(915) 263-6699

FEDERAL CORRECTIONAL INSTITUTION
2113 N Hwy 175, Seagoville, TX 75159
(972)287-2911

FEDERAL CORRECTIONAL INSTITUTION
PO Box 9500, 4001 FCI Rd., Texarkana, TX 75505-9500
(903) 838-4587

FEDERAL CORRECTIONAL INSTITUTION
PO Box 4000, 206 Thornton St., Three Rivers, TX 78071
(361) 786-3576

FEDERAL CORRECTIONAL INSTITUTION (Petersburg)
PO Box 1000, Petersburg, VA 23804-1000
(804) 733-7881

FEDERAL CORRECTIONAL INSTITUTION (Beckley)
PO Box 1280, Beaver, WV 25813
(304) 252-9758

FEDERAL CORRECTIONAL INSTITUTION
PO Box 1000, Greenbag Rd., Morgantown, WV 26507-1000
(304) 296-4416

FEDERAL CORRECTIONAL INSTITUTION
PO Box 500, off County Hwy G, Oxford, WI 53952-0500
(608) 584- 5511

FEDERAL PRISON CAMPS

FEDERAL PRISON CAMP
Maxwell Air Force Base, Montgomery, AL 36112
(334) 293-2100

FEDERAL PRISON CAMP
Eglin Air Force Base, PO Box 600, Eglin, FL 32542-7606
(850) 882-8522

FEDERAL PRISON CAMP
110 Raby Ave, Pensacola, FL 32509-5127
(850) 457-1911

FEDERAL PRISON CAMP
Oakdale, PO Box 5060, Oakdale, LA 71463
(318) 335-4466

FEDERAL PRISON CAMP
PO Box 1400, Stebner Rd, Duluth, MN 55814
(218) 722-8634

FEDERAL PRISON CAMP
Seymour Johnson Air Force Base, CB 8004, Bldg 3681, Goldsboro, NC 27533-8004
(919) 735-9711

FEDERAL PRISON CAMP
Allenwood, PO Box 1000, Rt 15, Montgomery, PA 17752
(570) 547-1641

FEDERAL PRISON CAMP
PO Box 1100 Douglas Ave, Yankton, SD 57078
(605) 665-3262

FEDERAL PRISON CAMP
PO Drawer 2197, 1100 Ursuline St, Bryan, TX 77805-2197
(409) 823-1879

FEDERAL PRISON CAMP
PO Box 16300, SSG Sims Rd, Bldg 11636, El Paso, TX 79906-0300
(915) 566-1271

FEDERAL PRISON CAMP
Glen Ray Rd, Box B, Rts 3 & 12, Alderson, WV 24910-0700
(304) 445-2901

FEDERAL DETENTION CENTERS

FEDERAL DETENTION CENTER
1705 E Hanna Rd, Eloy, AZ 85231
(520) 466-4141

FEDERAL DETENTION CENTER
PO Box 019118, Miami, FL 33101-9118
(305) 982-1114

FEDERAL DETENTION CENTER
PO Box 5060, E Whatley Rd, Oakdale, LA 71463-5060
(318) 335-4466

FEDERAL DETENTION CENTER
1200 Texas Ave, Houston, TX 77052-3505
(713) 221-5400

FEDERAL DETENTION CENTER
SeaTac, PO Box 13901, Seattle, WA 98198
(206) 870-5700

U.S. PAROLE COMMISSION

U.S. PAROLE COMMISSION
Central Office, 5550 Friendship Blvd, Ste 420, Chevy Chase, MD 20815-7286
(301) 492-5990

U.S. COURTS

FEDERAL CORRECTIONS OFFICE OF THE U.S. COURTS
One Columbus Circle NE, Washington, DC 20544
(202) 502-1620

U.S. AIR FORCE

CORRECTIONS DIVISION (HQ AFSFC/SPC)
(210) 671-0788

U.S. ARMY

U.S. ARMY CORRECTIONS SYSTEM
Headquarters Department of the Army (SAMO-ODL-O), Deputy Chief of Staff for
Operations & Plans, 400 Army Pentagon, Washington, DC 20301-0400
(703) 695-8481

U.S. NAVY

CORRECTIONS AND PROGRAMS DIVISION (NPC-84)
5720 Integrity Dr, Millington, TN 38055-8400
(901) 874-4442

U.S. MARINE CORPS

CORRECTIONS SECTION
Marine Corps Headquarters (CODE POS-40), Washington, DC 20380-1775
(703) 614-2674[12]

CHAPTER SEVEN

JUDICIAL INTERNSHIPS

CHAPTER SEVEN: JUDICIAL INTERNSHIPS

INTRODUCTION

This chapter presents the numerous internship opportunities within the judicial system—the courts. It commences with a crystal clear view of the judicial system in the United States and the roles of the major players. It will then discuss the various careers within the system that might be pursued by students who have a desire to become major players of the criminal justice system.

It is important to note the wide variety of job opportunities available within the judicial system. It is a highly complex and by nature an adversarial system. Within the criminal courts this adversarial system is played out as the state or government versus the defendant. The judicial process is so involved and full of loopholes and technicalities that the system demands a substantial number of employees to respond to complex matters.

The chapter will disclose conditions and employment statistics. Also, the roles and functions of the paralegal, court administrator, the criminal case managers and other court positions will be briefly covered,

CHAPTER OUTLINE

1. Conditions and Employment
2. Employment Statistics
3. Judicial Internships

   a. Court Administrator
   b. Paralegal
   c. Criminal Case Manager
   d. Court Reporter
   e. Bailiff
   f. Clerk

4. Courts

CONDITIONS AND EMPLOYMENT

The courts represent one of the more volatile areas of the criminal justice system. The court system includes not only one of the most competitive internship categories, but one of the most explosive in terms of overall growth rate—paralegal.

The criminal justice system is very complex and it needs a substantial number of players or participants. Once you are involved in your internship, the jobs may not seem as glamorous as they are frequently depicted in the media, but they are extremely important and provide exceptional career opportunities.

EMPLOYMENT STATISTICS

The forecast demand for paralegals, court administrators and other judicial support personnel is expected to increase a great deal from 2001 to 2010. It should be noted that while the court system must be examined as a uniform industry that responds as a single unit to economic, political and legal trends, in this context we must view each major internship category separately, and especially in the subsequent information.

JUDICIAL INTERNSHIPS

COURT ADMINISTRATOR

Description

Responsible for court administration and management, with regard to casework, court staffing and fiscal matters. Internships can be found at local, state and federal levels.

Requirements

Bachelor's degree, often requires graduate education
US citizen

Contact Information

National Center for State Courts
300 Newport Avenue
Williamsburg, VA   23185
(757) 253-2000

U.S. Office of Personnel Management
1900 E. Street NW
Washington, DC   20415
(202) 606-1800
www.opm.gov
Hotline: (912) 757-3000

PARALEGAL

Description

Paralegals assist lawyers in doing much of the background work for cases. Responsibilities include researching laws, prior cases, investigating facts and evidence, writing legal documents and briefs, coordinating communications and maintaining records of all documents.

Requirements

A college degree or a paralegal certificate from a two or four year program may be required. Collegiate or work-related experience. To become a certified legal assistant, applicants must pass a two-day examination administered by the National Association of Legal Assistants.

Contact Information

Contact the local, state or federal courts in your jurisdiction, U.S. Office of Personnel Management or law firms' directories.

U.S. Office of Personnel Management
1900 G. Street NW
Washington, DC   20415
(202) 606 1800
www.opm.gov
www.usajobs.opm.gov
(job listing)
Hotline: (912) 757-3000

CRIMINAL CASE MANAGER

Description

Responsibilities include the investigation of accused as it relates to bail and the amount of bail. Makes recommendation for pre-trial status, and completes the presentence investigation report.

Requirements

Bachelor's degree, often requires graduate education for the director of the criminal case manager's office or unit.

Contact Information

National Center for State Courts
300 Newport Avenue
Williamsburg, VA   23185
(757) 253-2000

U.S. Office of Personnel Management
1900 E. Street NW
Washington, DC   20415
(202) 606-1800
www.opm.gov
Hotline: (912) 757-3000

COURT REPORTER

Description

Court reporters work in courtrooms and outside the courtroom for legal and private organizations, documenting proceedings as official transcripts utilizing a stenotype machine or recording machine, which is fed into computer-aided transcriptions.

Requirements

Qualifying examination for state licensing, which includes testing on skills and knowledge, dictation and transcription. Many states require state certification which is a certified court reporter degree.

Two and four year programs at post-secondary technical and vocational schools.

Contact Information

Contact the local, state or federal court in your jurisdiction. Also check the U.S. Office of Personnel Management hotline at (912) 774-2299.

National Court Reporters Association
8224 Old Courthouse road
Vienna, VA   22182
www.verbatimreporters.com

National Center for State Courts
 300 Newport Avenue
Williamsburg, VA   23185
(757) 253-2000
www.ncsc.dni.us

BAILIFF

Description

Bailiffs are officers, usually deputy sheriffs, who are assigned to facilitate the court process. Duties of the bailiffs include maintaining order in the court and assisting in the moving of those involved in the court process, for example, defendants and the jury.

Requirements

The bailiffs are sworn officers and will possess all of the regular requirements as for any police officer. Nonsworn bailiffs may require less education or experience than a regular police officer.

Contact Information
Contact the local, state or federal court in your jurisdiction. Also check with the U.S. Office of Personnel Management hotline at (912) 774-2299.

CLERK

Description

The role of the clerk includes the maintaining of accurate records and ensuring that court schedules are made and enforced. It is the duty of the clerk to see that all records are properly maintained.

Requirements

Bachelor's degree
Two year education of post-secondary college
US. citizen

Contact Information

National Center for State Courts
300 Newport Avenue
Williamsburg, VA 23185
(757) 253-2000

U.S. Office of Personnel Management
1900 E. Street NW
Washington, DC   20415
(202) 606-1800
www.opm.gov
Hotline: (912) 757-3000

COURTS

U.S. SUPREME COURT

Chief Justice, 1 First St NE, Washington, DC 20543, (202) 479-3000

U.S. COURTS

ADMINISTRATIVE OFFICE

Director, 1 Columbus Cir NE, Washington, DC 20544, (202) 273-3000

U.S. DISTRICT COURTS

ALABAMA – MIDDLE

Chief Judge, PO Box 629, Montgomery, AL 36101, (334) 223-7802

ALABAMA – NORTHERN

Chief Judge, 1729 5th Ave N Rm 882, Birmingham, AL 35203, (205) 278-1800

ALABAMA – SOUTHERN

Chief Judge, 113 St Joseph St, Mobile, AL 36602, (334) 690-2175

ALASKA

Chief Judge, 222 W 7th Ave #41, Anchorage, AK 99513, (907) 271-3198

ARIZONA

Senior Judge, 230 N 1st Ave, Phoenix, AZ 85025, (602) 514-7225

ARKANSAS – EASTERN

Chief Judge, 600 W Capitol Ste 522, Little Rock, AR 72201, (501) 604-5100

ARKANSAS – WESTERN

Chief Judge, PO Box 3487, Fayetteville, AR 72702, (501) 444-7876

CALIFORNIA – CENTRAL

Clerk of Court, 312 N Spring St Rm G-8, Los Angeles, CA 90012, (213) 894-4445

CALIFORNIA – EASTERN

Chief Judge, 650 Capital Mall, Sacramento, CA 95814, (916) 930-4230

CALIFORNIA – NORTHERN

Chief Judge, 450 Golden Gate Ave 16th Fl Rm 16-1111, San Francisco, CA 94102, (415) 522-2000

CALIFORNIA – SOUTHERN

Chief Judge, 940 Front St Courtroom 1, San Diego, CA 92101, (619) 557-6016

COLORADO

Chief Judge, 1929 Stout St, Denver, CO 80294, (303) 844-4627

CONNECTICUT

Senior Judge, 208 US Cthse 141 Church St, New Haven, CT 06510, (203) 773-2105

DELAWARE

Chief Judge, 844 King St Lock Box 27, Wilmington, DE 19801, (302) 573-6155

DISTRICT OF COLUMBIA

Chief Judge, 333 Constitution Ave NW, E Barrett Prettyman Bldg, Washington, DC 20001, (202) 354-3500

FLORIDA – MIDDLE

Chief Judge, 801 N Florida Ave Ste 1730, Tampa, FL 33602, (813) 301-5730

FLORIDA – NORTHERN

Senior US District Judge, 110 E Park Ave, Tallahassee, FL 32301, (850) 942-8853

FLORIDA – SOUTHERN

Chief Judge, 90 NE Fourth St Ste 1155, Miami, FL 33132, (305) 523-5150

GEORGIA – MIDDLE

Chief Judge, PO Box 1014, Macon, GA 31202, (478) 752-3500

GEORGIA – NORTHERN

Chief Judge, 1988 US Cthse 75 Spring St SW, Atlanta, GA 30303, (404) 215-1490

GEORGIA – SOUTHERN

Chief Judge, PO Box 2106, Augusta, GA 30903, (706) 722-6074

HAWAII

Chief Judge, 300 Ala Moana Blvd, Rm C-400, Honolulu, HI 96850, (808) 541-1904

IDAHO

District Judge, 550 W Fort St Fed Bldg MSC 040, Boise, ID 83724, (208) 334-9270

ILLINOIS – CENTRAL

Chief Judge, 122 Fed Bldg 100 NE Monroe St, Peoria, IL 61602, (309) 671-7821

ILLINOIS – NORTHERN

Chief Judge, 219 S Dearborn St Rm 2548, Chicago, IL 60604, (312) 435-5600

ILLINOIS – SOUTHERN

Chief Judge, 301 W Main St, Benton, IL 62812, (618) 435-3779

INDIANA – NORTHERN

Chief Judge, 2145 Fed Bldg 1300 S Harrison St, Ft Wayne, IN 46802, (219) 422-2841

INDIANA – SOUTHERN

Chief Judge, 46 E Ohio St 210 US Cthse, Indianapolis, IN 46204, (317) 299-3600

IOWA – NORTHERN

Judge, 101 First St SE Fed Bldg Rm 304, Cedar Rapids, IA 52401, (319) 286-2330

IOWA – SOUTHERN

Chief Judge, 123 E Walnut St Rm 115, Des Moines, IA 50309, (515) 284-6235

KANSAS

Chief Judge, 500 State Ave Ste 529, Kansas City, KS 66101, (913) 551-6721

KENTUCKY – EASTERN

Chief Judge, 320 Fed Bldg 1405 Greenup Ave, Ashland, KY 41101, (606) 329-2592

KENTUCKY – WESTERN

Chief Judge, 601 W Broadway Rm 247, Louisville, KY 40202, (502) 625-3600

LOUISIANA – EASTERN

Chief Judge, 500 Camp St, New Orleans, LA 70130, (504) 589-7570

LOUISIANA – MIDDLE

Chief Judge, 777 Florida St Ste 313, Baton Rouge, LA 70801, (225) 389-3576

LOUISIANA – WESTERN

Chief Judge, PO Box 1031, Alexandria, LA 71309, (318) 473-7375

MAINE

Chief Judge, 156 Federal St, Portland, ME 04101, (207) 780-3280

MARYLAND

Chief Judge, 101 W Lombard St, Baltimore, MD 21201, (410) 962-0782

MASSACHUSETTS

Chief Judge, 1 Courthouse Way Ste 5170, Boston, MA 02210, (617) 748-9138

MICHIGAN – EASTERN

Chief Judge, 231 W Lafayette Blvd, Rm 730, Detroit, MI 48226, (313) 234-5110

MICHIGAN – WESTERN

Chief Judge, 410 W Michigan, Kalamazoo, MI 49007, (616) 343-7542

MINNESOTA

Chief Judge, 316 N Robert St, St Paul, MN 55101, (612) 664-5000

MISSISSIPPI – NORTHERN

Senior Judge, PO Box 925, Aberdeen, MS 39730, (662) 369-8307

MISSISSIPPI – SOUTHERN

Chief Judge, 245 E Capitol St, Ste 110, Jackson, MS 39201, (601) 965-4963

MISSOURI – EASTERN

Chief Judge, 1114 Market St US Cthse & Custom Hse, St Louis, MO 63101, (314) 539-3202

MISSOURI – WESTERN

Chief Judge, 400 E 9th US Cthse, Kansas City, MO 64106, (816) 512-5600

MONTANA

Chief Judge, PO Box 985, Billings, MT 59103, (406) 247-7011

NEBRASKA

Chief Judge, PO Box 1076, Omaha, NE 68101, (402) 221-3362

NEVADA

Chief Judge, 400 S Virginia St, Ste 708, Reno, NV 89501, (775) 686-5949

NEW HAMPSHIRE

Chief Judge, 55 Pleasant St, Concord, NH 03301, (603) 226-7303

NEW JERSEY

Chief Judge, 402 E State St, Rm 4000, Trenton, NJ 08608, (609) 989-2123

NEW MEXICO

Chief Judge, 333 Lomas Blvd, Albuquerque, NM 87102, (505) 348-2000

NEW YORK – EASTERN

Chief Judge, 225 Cadman Plz E, Brooklyn, NY 11201, (718) 260-2300

NEW YORK – NORTHERN

Chief Judge, US Court & Fed Bldg, 15 Henry St, Binghamton, NY 13902, (607) 773-2892

NEW YORK – SOUTHERN

Chief Judge, 300 Quarropas St, White Plains, NY 10601, (914) 390-4077

NEW YORK – WESTERN

Chief Judge, 2500 US Cthse, 100 State St, Rochester, NY 14614, (716) 263-5894

NORTH CAROLINA – EASTERN

Chief Judge, 306 E Main St, Fed Bldg 217, Elizabeth City, NC 27909, (252) 338-4033

NORTH CAROLINA – MIDDLE

Senior Judge, 223-A Fed Bldg, 251 N Main St, Winston-Salem, NC 27101, (336) 631-5007

NORTH CAROLINA – WESTERN

Chief Judge, 401 W Trade St, 195 Charles R Jonas Fed Bldg, Charlotte, NC 28202, (704) 350-7440

NORTH DAKOTA

District Judge, PO Box 1578, Bismarck, ND 58502, (701) 530-2315

OHIO – NORTHERN

Chief Judge, 201 Superior Ave E, Cleveland, OH 44114, (216) 522-8251

OHIO – SOUTHERN

Chief Judge, 200 W 2nd St, Dayton, OH 45402, (937) 512-1500

OKLAHOMA – EASTERN

Chief Judge, PO Box 2999, Muskogee, OK 74402, (918) 687-2405

OKLAHOMA – NORTHERN

Senior Judge, 224 S Boulder, Rm 210, Tulsa, OK 74103, (918) 581-7966

OKLAHOMA – WESTERN

Chief Judge, 3309 US Cthse, 200 NW 4th St, Oklahoma City, OK 73102, (405) 231-5554

OREGON

Chief Judge, Rm 240 US Cthse, 211 E 7th Ave, Eugene, OR 97401, (541) 465-6773

PENNSYLVANIA – EASTERN

Chief Judge, 601 Market St, Rm 17614, Philadelphia, PA 19106, (215) 597-0692

PENNSYLVANIA – MIDDLE

Chief Judge, PO Box 913, Scranton, PA 18501, (570) 207-5720

PENNSYLVANIA – WESTERN

Senior Judge, US PO & Cthse Rm 803, Pittsburgh, PA 15219, (412) 208-7380

PUERTO RICO

Chief Judge, 150 Carlos Chardon Ave Fed Bldg, San Juan, PR 00918, (787) 772-3130

RHODE ISLAND

Chief Judge, 214B US Cthse One Exchange Terrace, Providence, RI 02903, (401) 752-7060

SOUTH CAROLINA

Senior District Judge, PO Box 835, Charleston, SC 29402, (843) 579-1490

SOUTH DAKOTA

Chief Judge, 400 S Phillips, Rm 202, Sioux Falls, SD 57104, (605) 330-4505

TENNESSEE – EASTERN

District Judge, PO Box 2484, Knoxville, TN 37901, (865) 545-4215

TENNESSEE – MIDDLE

Chief Judge, 824 US Cthse, 801 Broadway, Nashville, TN 37203, (615) 736-2774

TENNESSEE – WESTERN

Chief Judge, 167 N Main St Ste 1157, Memphis, TN 38103, (901) 495-1265

TEXAS – EASTERN

Chief Judge, 300 Willow Jack Brooks Fed Bldg Ste 239, Beaumont, TX 77701, (409) 654-2880

TEXAS – NORTHERN

Chief Judge, 1100 Commerce St 15th Fl, Dallas, TX 75242, (214) 753-2295

TEXAS – SOUTHERN

Chief Judge, PO Box 1060, Laredo, TX 78042, (956) 726-2267

TEXAS – WESTERN

Chief Judge, 200 W 8th St, Austin, TX 78701, (512) 916-5675

UTAH

Senior Judge, 148 US Cthse, 350 S Main St, Salt Lake City, UT 84101, (801) 524-6190

VERMONT

Chief Judge, PO Box 760, Brattleboro, VT 05302, (802) 258-4413

VIRGIN ISLANDS

Chief Judge, 3013 Estate Golden Rock, St Croix, VI 00820-4355, (340) 773-5021

VIRGINIA – EASTERN

Chief Judge, 401 Courthouse Sq, Alexandria, VA 22314, (703) 299-2112

VIRGINIA – WESTERN

Chief Judge, PO Box 2421, Roanoke, VA 24010, (540) 857-5120

WASHINGTON – EASTERN

Chief Judge, PO Box 2208, Spokane, WA 99210, (509) 353-3163

WASHINGTON – WESTERN

Judge, 1010 Fifth Ave, Seattle, WA 98104, (206) 553-2469

WEST VIRGINIA – NORTHERN

Chief Judge, PO Box 791, Wheeling, WV 26003, (304) 233-1120

WEST VIRGINIA – SOUTHERN

Chief Judge, PO Box 351, Charleston, WV 25322, (304) 347-3100

WISCONSIN – EASTERN

Chief Judge, 517 E Wisconsin Ave, 471 US Cthse, Milwaukee, WI 53202, (414) 297-1122

WISCONSIN – WESTERN

Chief Judge, PO Box 591, Madison, WI 53701, (608) 264-5504

WYOMING

US District Judge, PO Box 985, Cheyenne, WY 82003, (307) 634-6072

COURT OF APPEALS

DISTRICT OF COLUMBIA CIRCUIT: WASHINGTON DC

Chief Judge, E Barrett Prettyman Cthse, 333 Constitution Ave NW, Washington, DC 20001, (202) 216-7380

FIRST CIRCUIT: MAINE, MASSACHUSETTS, NEW HAMPSHIRE, PUERTO RICO, RHODE ISLAND

Senior Judge, 1618 John W McCormack PO & Cthse Bldg, Boston, MA 02109, (617) 223-9049

SECOND CIRCUIT: CONNECTICUT, NEW YORK, VERMONT

Senior Judge, PO Box 696, Brattleboro, VT 05302, (802) 254-5000

THIRD CIRCUIT: DELAWARE, NEW JERSEY, PENNSYLVANIA, VIRGIN ISLANDS

Chief Judge, US Cthse, 601 Market St Rm 19613, Philadelphia, PA 19106, (215) 597-9642

FOURTH CIRCUIT: MARYLAND, NORTH CAROLINA, SOUTH CAROLINA, VIRGINIA, WEST VIRGINIA

Chief Judge, Rm 230 US Cthse, 255 W Main St, Charlottesville, NC 22902, (804) 296-7063

FIFTH CIRCUIT: LOUISIANA, MISSISSIPPI, TEXAS

Chief Judge, US Cthse Rm 11020, 515 Rusk Ave, Houston, TX 77002, (713) 250-5750

SIXTH CIRCUIT: KENTUCKY, MICHIGAN, OHIO, TENNESSEE

Circuit Judge, 640 Fed Bldg, 110 Michigan St NW, Grand Rapids, MI 49503, (616) 456-2551

SEVENTH CIRCUIT: ILLINOIS, INDIANA, WISCONSIN

Chief Judge, 219 S Dearborn St Rm 2788F, Chicago, IL 60604, (312) 435-5806

EIGHTH CIRCUIT: ARKANSAS, IOWA, MINNESOTA, MISSOURI, NEBRASKA, NORTH DAKOTA, SOUTH DAKOTA

Chief Judge, 311 US Cthse 400 S Phillips Ave, Saux Falls, SD 57104, (816) 512-5800

NINTH CIRCUIT: ALASKA, ARIZONA, CALIFORNIA, GUAM, HAWAII, IDAHO, MONTANA, NEVADA, NORTHERN MARIANA ISLANDS, OREGON, WASHINGTON

Chief Justice, 400 S Virginia St Ste 708, Reno, NV 89501, (775) 686-5949

TENTH CIRCUIT: COLORADO, KANSAS, NEW MEXICO, OKLAHOMA, UTAH, WYOMING

Senior Circuit Judge, 6012 Fed Bldg, Salt Lake City, UT 84138, (801) 524-5252

ELEVENTH CIRCUIT: ALABAMA, FLORIDA, GEORGIA

Circuit Judge, PO Box 53135, Jacksonville, FL 32201, (904) 232-2496

U.S. DEPARTMENT OF JUSTICE

OFFICE OF ATTORNEY GENERAL

Attorney General, 950 Pennsylvania Ave NW Rm 4545, Washington, DC 20530, (202) 514-2001

U.S. ATTORNEYS

EXECUTIVE OFFICE FOR THE U.S. ATTORNEY

Director, 950 Pennsylvania Ave NW, Washington, DC 20530, (202) 514-2121

ALABAMA – MIDDLE

US Attorney, PO Box 197, Montgomery, AL 36101, (334) 223-7280

ALABAMA – NORTH

US Attorney, 200 Fed Bldg, 1800 5th Ave N, Birmingham, AL 35203, (205) 244-2001

ALABAMA – SOUTH

US Attorney, 63 S Royal St Ste 600, Mobile, AL 36602, (334) 441-5845

ALASKA

US Attorney, Rm 253 Fed Bldg & Cthse, 222 W 7th Ave #9, Anchorage, AK 99513, (907) 271-5071

Assistant US Attorney, 101 12th Ave Box 2 Rm 310, Fairbanks, AK 99701, (907) 456-0245

ARIZONA

US Attorney, Rm 4000 Fed Bldg, 230 N 1st Ave, Phoenix, AZ 85025, (602) 514-7500

1st Assistant US Attorney, 110 S Church Ave Ste 8310, Tucson, AZ 85701, (520) 620-7300

ARKANSAS – EAST

US Attorney, 425 W Capital 5th Fl, Little Rock, AR 72203, (501) 324-5342

ARKANSAS – WEST

US Attorney, PO Box 1524, Fort Smith, AR 72902, (501) 783-5125

CALIFORNIA – CENTRAL

US Attorney, 312 N Spring St 12th Fl, Los Angeles, CA 90012, (213) 894-4600

Chief, Santa Ana Beach, 411 W Fourth St Ste 8000, Santa Ana, CA 92701, (714) 338-3500

CALIFORNIA – EAST

US Attorney, 501 I Ste 10-100, Sacramento, CA 95814, (916) 554-2700

Chief of Criminal Division, 1130 O St Rm 3654, Fresno, CA 93721, (559) 498-7272

CALIFORNIA – NORTH

US Attorney, 450 Golden Gate Ave, San Francisco, CA 94102, (415) 436-7200

CALIFORNIA – SOUTH

US Attorney, 880 Front St Ste 6293, San Diego, CA 92101, (619) 557-5610

COLORADO

US Attorney, 1961 Stout St Ste 1200, Denver, CO 80294, (303) 844-2081

CONNECTICUT

US Attorney, 157 Church St 23 Fl, New Haven, CT 06510, (203) 821-3700

Supervising US Attorney, 450 Main St Fed Bldg Rm 328, Hartford, CT 06103, (860) 947-1101

Supervisor, Rm 309 Fed Bldg, 915 Lafayette Blvd, Bridgeport, CT 06604, (203) 696-3000

DELAWARE

US Attorney, 1201 Market St Ste 1100, Wilmington, DE 19899, (302) 573-6277

DISTRICT OF COLUMBIA

Law Enforcement Coordinator, 555 4th St NW Judiciary Ctr Bldg, Washington, DC 20001, (202) 514-7483

FLORIDA – MIDDLE

US Attorney, 400 N Tampa St Ste 3200, Tampa, FL 33602, (813) 274-6000

Managing Assistant US Attorney, PO Box 600, Jacksonville, FL 32201, (904) 232-2682

Acting Managing Assistant US Attorney, 201 Fed Bldg, 80 N Hughey Ave, Orlando, FL 32801, (407) 648-6700

Managing Assistant US Attorney, 2110 First St Ste 3-137, Fort Myers, FL 33901, (941) 461-2200

FLORIDA – NORTH

US Attorney, 111 N Adams St 4th Fl, Tallahassee, FL 32301, (850) 942-8430

US Attorney, 21 E Garden St, Pensacola, FL 32501, (850) 444-4000

US Attorney, 104 N Main St, Gainesville, FL 32601, (352) 378-0996

FLORIDA – SOUTH

US Attorney, 99 NE 4th St, Miami, FL 33132, (305) 961-9000

Managing Assistant US Attorney, 500 E Broward Blvd, Fort Lauderdale, FL 33394, (954) 356-7255

Managing Supervisor, 500 Australian Ave Ste 400, West Palm Beach, FL 33401, (561) 820-8711

Chief Assistant US Attorney, 505 S 2nd St Ste 200, Fort Pierce, FL 34950, (561) 466-0899

GEORGIA – MIDDLE

US Attorney, PO Box U, Macon, GA 31202, (478) 752-3511

GEORGIA – NORTH

US Attorney, 1800 US Cthse, 75 Spring St SW, Atlanta, GA 30303, (404) 581-6000

GEORGIA – SOUTH

US Attorney, 100 Bull St, Savannah, GA 31401, (912) 652-4422

1st Assistant US Attorney, PO Box 2017, Augusta, GA 30903, (706) 724-0517

HAWAII

US Attorney, 300 Ala Moana Blvd Rm 6-100, Honolulu, HI 96850, (808) 541-2850

IDAHO

US Attorney, PO Box 32, Boise, ID 83707, (208) 334-1211

ILLINOIS – CENTRAL

US Attorney, 600 E Monroe St Rm 312, Springfield, IL 62701, (217) 492-4450

US Attorney, 1830 2nd Ave Ste 320, Rock Island, IL 62701, (309) 793-5884

US Attorney, 201 S Vine St Ste 226, Urbana, IL 61801, (217) 373-5875

US Attorney, 100 NE Monroe St, Peoria, IL 61602, (309) 671-7050

ILLINOIS – NORTH

US Attorney, 219 S Dearborn St 5th Fl, Chicago, IL 60604, (312) 353-5300

US Attorney, 308 W State St Rm 300, Rockford, IL 61101, (815) 987-4444

ILLINOIS – SOUTH

US Attorney, 9 Executive Dr Ste 300, Fairview Hts, IL 62208, (618) 628-3700

US Attorney, 402 W Main St Ste 2A, Benton, IL 62812, (618) 439-3808

INDIANA – NORTH

US Attorney, 1001 Main St Ste A, Dyer, IN 46311, (219) 322-8576

Assistant US Attorney, M01 Robert A Grant Fed Bldg, 204 S Main St, South Bend, IN 46601, (219) 236-8287

Assistant US Attorney, 3128 Fed Bldg, 1300 S Harrison St, Fort Wayne, IN 46802, (219) 226-6333

INDIANA – SOUTH

US Attorney, US Cthse 5th Fl, 46 E Ohio St, Indianapolis, IN 46204, (317) 226-6333

IOWA – NORTH

US Attorney, 401 First St SE Ste 400, Cedar Rapids, IA 52401, (319) 363-6333

Chief Assistant US Attorney, 320 6th St Ste 203, Sioux City, IA 51101, (712) 255-6011

IOWA – SOUTH

US Attorney, 110 E Court Ave, US Cthse Annex Ste 286, Des Moines, IA 50309, (515) 284-6257

KANSAS

US Attorney, 1200 Epic Ctr, 301 N Main St, Wichita, KS 67202, (316) 269-6481

Assistant US Attorney, 444 Quincy St Rm 290, Topeka, KS 66683, (785) 295-2850

Assistant US Attorney, 500 State Ave Rm 360, Kansas City, KS 66101, (913) 551-6730

KENTUCKY – EAST

US Attorney, 110 W Vine St Ste 400, Lexington, KY 40507, (859) 233-2661

V PO Box 72, Covington, KY 41012, (859) 655-3200

KENTUCKY – WEST

US Attorney, 510 W Broadway 10th Fl, Louisville, KY 40202, (502) 582-5911

LOUISIANA – EAST

US Attorney, 501 Magazine St 2nd Fl, New Orleans, LA 70130, (504) 680-3000

LOUISIANA – MIDDLE

US Attorney, 777 Florida St, 208 Russell B Long Fed Bldg, Baton Rouge, LA 70801, (225) 389-0443

LOUISIANA – WEST

US Attorney, 300 Fannin St Ste 3201, Shreveport, LA 71101, (318) 676-3600

Assistant US Attorney, 800 Lafayette St Ste 2200, Lafayette, LA 70501, (337) 262-6618

MAINE

US Attorney, PO Box 2460, Bangor, ME 04402, (207) 780-3257

US Attorney, 99 Franklin St 2nd Fl, Bangor, ME 04401, 9207) 945-0374

MARYLAND

US Attorney, 6625 US Cthse, 101 W Lombard St, Baltimore, MD 21201, (410) 209-4800

MASSACHUSETTS

US Attorney, 1 Cthse Way, US Cthse Ste 9200, Boston, MA 02210, (617) 748-3100

Assistant US Attorney, 1550 Main St, Rm 310 US Cthse, Springfield, MA 01103, (413) 785-0235

MICHIGAN – EAST

US Attorney, 211 W Fort St Ste 2001, Detroit, MI 48226, (313) 226-9504

Assistant US Attorney, 101 1st St Ste 200, Bay City, MI 48707, (989) 895-5712

Assistant US Attorney, 600 Church St, Flint, MI 48502, (810) 766-5031

MICHIGAN – WEST

US Attorney, PO Box 208, Grand Rapids, MI 49501, (616) 456-2404

Assistant US Attorney, 1930 US 41 W, Marquette, MI 49855, (906) 226-2500

MINNESOTA

US Attorney, 300 S 4th St Rm 600, Minneapolis MN 55415, (612) 664-5600

US Attorney, 316 N Robert St, St Paul, MN 55101, (952) 290-4401

MISSISSIPPI – NORTH

US Attorney, PO Box 886, Oxford, MS 38655, (662) 234-3351

MISSISSIPPI – SOUTH

US Attorney, 188 E Capitol St Ste 500, Jackson, MS 39201, (601) 965-4480

US Attorney, 808 Vieux Marche 2nd Fl, Biloxi, MS 39530, (228) 432-5521

MISSOURI – EAST

US Attorney, US Court & Custom Hse, 1114 Market St Rm 401, St Louis, MO 63101, (314) 539-2200

MISSOURI – WEST

US Attorney, 400 E 9th St 5th St, Kansas City, MO 64106, (816) 426-3122

Deputy US Attorney, 901 St Louis St Ste 500, Springfield, MO 65806, (417) 831-4406

Special Assistant US Attorney, 301 E McCarty Ste 100, Jefferson City, MO 65101, (573) 634-8214

MONTANA

US Attorney, 2929 Third Ave N Ste 400, Billings, MT 59101, (406) 657-6101

Assistant US Attorney, PO Box 3447, Great Falls, MT 59403, (406) 761-7715

Assistant US Attorney, 100 N Park Ave Ste 100, Helena, MT 59601, (406) 449-5370

NEBRASKA

US Attorney, 1620 Dodge St Ste 1400, Omaha, NE 68102, (402) 221-4774

US Attorney, 487 Fed Bldg, 100 Centennial Mall N, Lincoln, NE 68508, 9402) 437-5241

NEVADA

US Attorney, 701 E Bridger Ave Ste 800, Las Vegas, NV 89101, (702) 388-6336

US Attorney, 701 E Bridger Ave Ste 600, Las Vegas, NV 89101, (702) 388-6336

NEW HAMPSHIRE

US Attorney, 55 Pleasant St Rm 352, Concord, NH 03301, (603) 225-1552

NEW JERSEY

US Attorney, 970 Broad St, Fed Bldg 7th Fl, Newark, NJ 07102, (973) 645-2700

Assistant US Attorney, 401 Market 4th Fl, Camden, NJ 08101, (856) 757-5026

Assistant US Attorney, 402 E State St Rm 430, Trenton, NJ 08608, (609) 989-2190

NEW MEXICO

US Attorney, PO Box 607, Albuquerque, NM 87103, (505) 766-3341

Branch Chief, 555 S Belshor Ste 300, Las Cruces, NM 88011, (505) 522-2304

NEW YORK – EAST

US Attorney, 1 Pierpont Plz 15th Fl, Brooklyn, NY 11201, (718) 254-7000

Assistant US Attorney, (516) 228-8630

Chief, 825 E Gate Blvd Ste 301, Garden City, NY 11530, (516) 288-8630

NEW YORK – NORTH

US Attorney, 100 S Clinton St, Syracuse, NY 13261, (315) 448-0672

Assistant US Attorney, 445 Broadway, Rm 231 James P Foley US Cthse, Albany, NY 12207, (518) 431-0247

Supervisor Assistant US Attorney, 319 Fed Bldg, 15 Henry St, Binghamton, NY 13901, (607) 773-2887

NEW YORK – SOUTH

US Attorney, 1 St Andrews Plz, New York, NY 10007, (212) 637-2200

Assistant US Attorney in Charge, 300 Quarropas St, White Plains, NY 10601, (914) 993-1900

NEW YORK – WEST

US Attorney, 138 Delaware Ave, Buffalo, NY 14202, (716) 551-4811

Assistant US Attorney in Charge, 100 State St, 620 Fed Bldg, Rochester, NY 14614, (716) 262-6760

NORTH CAROLINA – EAST

US Attorney, 310 New Bern Ave Ste 800 Fed Bldg, Raleigh, NC 27601, (919) 856-4530

NORTH CAROLINA – MIDDLE

US Attorney, PO Box 1858, Greensboro, NC 27402, (336) 333-5351

NORTH CAROLINA – WEST

US Attorney, 227 W Trade St #1700, Charlotte, NC 28202, (704) 344-6222

Senior Litigation Counselor, 100 Otis St Rm 233, Asheville, NC 28801, (828) 271-4661

NORTH DAKOTA

US Attorney, Quentin Burdick Cthse, 655 1st Ave N Ste 250, Fargo, ND 85102, (701) 297-7400

Assistant US Attorney, PO Box 699, Bismarck, ND 58502, (701) 530-2420

OHIO – NORTH

US Attorney, 1800 Bank One Ctr, 600 Superior Ave E, Cleveland, OH 44114, (216) 622-3600

Supervisor Assistant US Attorney, Four Seagate Ste 308, Toledo, OH 43604, 9419) 259-6376

Supervisor Assistant US Attorney, 208 Fed Bldg, 2 S Main St, Akron, OH 44308, (330) 375-5716

OHIO – SOUTH

US Attorney, 280 N High St 4th Fl, Columbus, OH 43215, (614) 469-5715

Supervisor Assistant US Attorney, 220 Potter Stewart Cthse, 100 E 5th St, Cincinnati, OH 45202, (513) 684-3711

Senior Assistant US Attorney, 200 W Second St Rm 602, Dayton, OH 45402, (937) 225-2910

OKLAHOMA – EAST

US Attorney, 1200 W Okmulgee, Muskogee, OK 74401, (918) 684-5100

OKLAHOMA – NORTH

US Attorney, 333 W Fourth St Ste 3460, Tulsa, OK 74103, (918) 581-7463

OKLAHOMA – WEST

US Attorney, 210 W Park Ave Ste 400, Oklahoma City, OK 73102, (405) 553-8700

OREGON

US Attorney, 1000 SW 3rd Ave Ste 600, Portland, OR 97204, (503) 727-1000

Assistant US Attorney, 701 High St, Eugene, OR 97401, (541) 465-6771

PENNSYLVANIA – EAST

US Attorney, 615 Chestnut St Ste 1250, Philadelphia, PA 19106, (215) 861-8200

PENNSYLVANIA – MIDDLE

US Attorney, PO Box 309, Scranton, PA 18501, (570) 348-2800

US Attorney, Rm 220 Fed Bldg, 3rd & Walnut Sts, Harrisburg, PA 17108, (717) 221-4482

PENNSYLVANIA – WEST

US Attorney, 633 US PO & Cthse, 7th Ave & Grant St, Pittsburgh, PA 15219, (412) 644-3500

Assistant US Attorney, 100 State St #302, Erie, PA 16507, (814) 452-2906

Assistant US Attorney, Ste 224 Penn Traffic Bldg, Johnstown, PA 15901, (814) 533-4547

PUERTO RICO

US Attorney, Fed Bldg Rm 452 Chardon Ave, Alto Rey, PR 00918, (787) 766-5656

RHODE ISLAND

US Attorney, Ste Ctr 50 Kennedy Dr 8th Fl, Providence, RI 02903, (401) 528-5477

SOUTH CAROLINA

US Attorney, 1441 Main St Ste 500, Columbia, SC 29201, (803) 929-3000

Assistant US Attorney, PO Box 978, Charleston, SC 29402, (843) 727-4381

Assistant US Attorney, 105 N Spring St Ste 200, Greenville, SC 29601, (864) 282-2100

Assistant US Attorney, 401 W Evans St Rm 222, Florence, SC 29503, (843) 665-6688

SOUTH DAKOTA

US Attorney, PO Box 5073, Sioux Falls, SD 57117, (605) 330-4400

Supervisor Assistant US Attorney, 201 Fed Bldg, 515 9th St, Rapid City, SD 57701, (605) 342-7822

Supervisor Assistant US Attorney, 225 S Pierre St Rm 337, Pierre, SD 57501, (605) 224-5402

TENNESSEE – EAST

US Attorney, 800 Market St Ste 211, Knoxville, TN 37902, (865) 545-4167

Supervisor Assistant US Attorney, 1110 Market St Ste 301, Chattanooga, TN 37402, (423) 752-5140

Supervisor Assistant US Attorney, 103 W Summer St, Greenville, TN 37743, (423) 639-6759

Assistant US Attorney, 208 Sunset Dr Ste 509, Johnson City, TN 37604, (423) 282-1889

TENNESSEE – MIDDLE

US Attorney, 110 9th Ave S Ste A961, Nashville, TN 37203, (615) 736-5151

TENNESSEE – WEST

US Attorney, Rm 800 Fed Bldg 167 N Main St, Memphis, TN 38103, (901) 544-4231

Supervisor Assistant US Attorney, 109 S Highland Ave Ste 300, Jackson, TN 38301, (901) 422-6220

TEXAS – EAST

US Attorney, 350 Magnolia St Ste 150, Beaumont, TX 77701, (409) 839-2538

Assistant US Attorney, 110 N College Ave Ste 700, Tyler, TX 75702, (903) 590-1400

Executive Assistant US Attorney, One Grand Ctr Ste 500, Sherman, TX 75090, (903) 868-9454

Assistant US Attorney, 660 N Central Expy Ste 400, Plano, TX 75074, (972) 509-1201

Assistant US Attorney, Ward R Burke Fed Bldg, 104 N 3rd St Rm 001, Lufkin, TX 75901, (936) 639-8671

TEXAS – NORTH

US Attorney, 1100 Commerce St 3rd Fl, Dallas, TX 75242, (214) 659-8600

Executive Assistant US Attorney, 801 Cherry St Ste 1700, Fort Worth, TX 76102, (817) 252-5200

Deputy Criminal Chief, 1205 Texas Ave, Mahon Fed Bldg Ste 700, Lubbock, TX 79401, (806) 472-7351

TEXAS – SOUTH

US Attorney, 910 Travis Ste 1500, Houston, TX 77208, (713) 567-9300

Assistant US Attorney, 600 E Harrison St Rm 201, Brownsville, TX 78520, (956) 548-2554

Assistant US Attorney in Charge, 1100 Matamoras Ste 200, Laredo, TX 78042, (956) 723-6523

Assistant US Attorney, 606 N Carancahua St Ste 1400, Corpus Christi, TX 78476, (361) 888-3111

Assistant US Attorney in Charge, 1701 W Hwy 83 Ste 600, McAllen, TX 78501, (956) 618-8010

TEXAS – WEST

US Attorney, 601 NW Loop 410 Ste 600, San Antonio, TX 78216, (210) 384-7100

Chief Assistant US Attorney, 700 E San Antonio St Ste 200, El Paso, TX 79901, (915) 534-6884

Chief Assistant US Attorney, 816 Congress Ave Ste 1000, Austin, TX 78701, (512) 916-5858

Chief Prosecutor, 400 W Illinois Ste 1200, Midland, TX 79702, (915) 686-4110

Chief Assistant US Attorney, 700 University Parks Dr Ste 770, Waco, TX 76706, (254) 750-1580

Acting Chief Assistant US Attorney, 111 E Broadway 3rd Fl Rm 306, Del Rio, TX 78840, (830) 703-2025

UTAH

US Attorney, 185 S State St Ste 400, Salt Lake City, UT 84111, (801) 524-5682

VERMONT

US Attorney, 11 Elmwood Ave, Burlington, VT 05402, (802) 951-6725

VIRGIN ISLANDS

US Attorney, 5500 Veterans Dr Rm 260, St Thomas, VI 00802, (340) 774-5757

Managing Assistant US Attorney, 1108 King St Ste 201, St Croix, VI 00820, (340) 773-3920

VIRGINIA – EAST

US Attorney, 2100 Jamieson Ave, Alexandria, VA 22314, (703) 229-3700

Managing Assistant US Attorney, 600 E Main St Ste 1800, Richmond, VA 23219, (804) 819-5400

Supervisor Assistant US Attorney, 101 W Main St, World Trade Ctr Ste 8000, Norfolk, VA 23510, (757) 441-6331

VIRGINIA – WEST

US Attorney, PO Box 1709, Roanoke, VA 24008, (540) 857-2250

Managing Assistant US Attorney, PO Box 1098, Abingdon, VA 24212, (540) 628-4161

Managing Assistant US Attorney, 255 W Main St Rm 104, Charlottesville, VA 22902, (804) 293-4283

WASHINGTON – EAST

US Attorney, 920 W Riverside Ave Ste 300, Spokane, WA 99201, (509) 353-2767

Supervisor Assistant US Attorney, 402 E Yakima Ave Ste 210, Yakima, WA 98901, (509) 454-4425

WASHINGTON – WEST

US Attorney, 601 Union St Ste 5100, Seattle, WA 98101, (206) 553-7970

US Attorney, 1201 Pacific Ave Ste 450, Tacoma, WA 98402, (253) 428-3800

WEST VIRGINIA – NORTH

Assistant US Attorney, PO Box 591, Wheeling, WV 26003, (304) 234-0100

Assistant US Attorney, PO Box 190, Elkins, WV 26241, (304) 636-1739

1st Assistant US Attorney, 320 W Pike St #300, Clarksburg, WV 26301, (304) 623-7030

WEST VIRGINIA – SOUTH

US Attorney, PO Box 1713, Charleston, WV 25326, (304) 345-2200

US Attorney, PO Box 1239, Huntington, WV 25714, (304) 529-5799

WISCONSIN – EAST

US Attorney, 530 Fed Bldg, 517 E Wisconsin Ave, Milwaukee, WI 53202, (414) 297-1700

WISCONSIN – WEST

US Attorney, 660 W Washington Ave Ste 200, Madison, WI 53701, (608) 264-5158

WYOMING

US Attorney, PO Box 668, Cheyenne, WY 82003, (307) 772-2124

Assistant US Attorney Criminal Chief, 111 S Wolcott Rm 300, Casper, WY 82601, (307) 261-5434

Assistant US Attorney, 933 Main, Lander, WY 82520, (307) 332-8195[13]

CHAPTER EIGHT

TRENDS/VISIONS

CHAPTER EIGHT: TRENDS/VISIONS

Technology is changing the scope and breadth of the criminal justice system. The 2010 and plus years will be facing new demands to confront the emerging internship opportunities.

The juvenile corrections trends will vary from state to state, but the overall national demand for juvenile correction officers and social workers will continue to grow.

The drug courts represent a new kind of opportunity for judicial and correctional professionals. The Drug Courts Program Office has awarded more than 50 million dollars to approximately 300 jurisdictions for the planning, implementation or development of drug courts. This can easily be interpreted into an extensive growth for social workers and other judicial and correctional workers who specialize in substance abuse treatment and related programs.[14]

There is a substantial increase in the jail population for the adult and juvenile offenders. This rapid increase has forced the criminal justice system to examine home detention as a practical alternative to incarceration. By keeping the offenders at home, the electronic-monitoring technology has provided a way to ease the overcrowding of the jails and prisons. The electronic monitoring is often used in conjunction with home detention, offering an effective, inexpensive method of supervising probationers.

The demand for the new areas of corrections and related fields are represented in the following types of opportunities:

1. Safety Manager: offers technical advice on or manages occupational safety programs, regulations and standards.

2. Ombudsman: acts as an unbiased liaison between inmates and facility administration; investigates inmate complaints, reports findings and helps achieve equitable settlements of disputes between the inmates and the correctional administration.

3. Computer Specialist: manages or designs use and maintenance of computer systems. This is an area of great need in the law enforcement, corrections and judicial fields.

4. Substance Abuse Specialist: manages or designs substance abuse treatments in order to counter the new or designer drugs.

The above are just a few examples of the emerging trends in the criminal justice system.

Technology will continue to play an important role in the operations of public and private sector organizations combating crime. Moreover, advances in technology (e.g., cellular phones) and the lowered cost of using technology will allow more people to use these tools. This, of course, also applies to criminals, as they will be better able to afford the equipment necessary for committing check fraud, identity theft and counterfeit documents.

The increase in electronic commerce over the internet will provide new opportunities for crime. The availability of information on the internet has already increased the volume of crime.

While the data is not complete, there is a clear trend toward an increase in technology-based crime.

CHAPTER NINE

CRIMINAL JUSTICE
DEGREE PROGRAMS

CHAPTER NINE: CRIMINAL JUSTICE DEGREE PROGRAMS

CONTINUING YOUR EDUCATION

The two year degree or the associate degree will provide the criminal justice major with the opportunity to secure a fulltime position in the field, or after a few years of criminal justice related experience. It is important for the criminal justice major that the student should have career goals that include the completion of the Bachelor of Arts or Science degrees in criminal justice. The criminal justice majors may be interested in the following list of four (4) year degree programs throughout the United States.

THE FOLLOWING COLLEGES/UNIVERSITIES OFFER THE BACHELOR'S DEGREE IN CRIMINAL JUSTICE

Aims College, Criminal Justice Department, Greeley, CO 80632, (970) 330-8008

Alabama State University, Department of Sociology and Criminal Justice, Montgomery, AL 36101, (334) 229-4120

Alfred University, Criminal Justice Studies, Alfred, NY 14802, (607) 871-2215

Alvernia College, Criminal Justice Department, Reading, PA 19607, (610) 796-8230

American University, Department of Justice, Law and Society, Washington, DC 20016, (202) 885-2956

Appalachian State University, Department of Political Sciences and Criminal Justice, Boone, NC 28608-2107, (828) 262-3085

Arkansas State University, Department of Criminology, Sociology, Social Work, and Geography, Jonesboro, AR 72467-2410, (501) 972-3705

Arizona State University, School of Justice Studies, Tempe, AZ 85287-0403, (602) 965-7085

Arizona State University West, Administration of Justice Department, Phoenix, AZ 85069-7100, (602) 543-6630

Armstrong Atlantic State University, Department of Criminal Justice, Social and Political Science, Savannah, GA 31419-1997, (912) 921-5677

Auburn University, Criminal Justice Department, Auburn, AL 36849, (334) 844-6054

Bakersfield College, Criminal Justice Department, Bakersfield, CA 93306, (805) 395-4481

Ball State University, Department of Criminal Justice and Criminology, North Quad, Muncie, IN 47306, (765) 285-5979

Becker College, Criminal Justice Administration Program, Millbury, MA 01527, (508) 791-9241

Bellevue University, Criminal Justice Administration, Fred H. Hawkins College, Bellevue, NE 68805, (402) 293-2038

Bemidji State University, Criminal Justice Department, Bemidji, MN 56601, (218) 755-2833

Boise State University, Department of Criminal Justice Administration, Boise, ID 83725-1955, (208) 426-4162

Bowling Green State University, Criminal Justice Program, Bowling Green, OH 43403, (419) 372-7778

Buffalo State College, Department of Criminal Justice, Buffalo, NY 14222, (716) 878-6138

Caldwell College, Department of Sociology and Criminal Justice, Caldwell, NJ 07006, (973) 228-4424

California State University, Criminal Justice Department, Sacramento, CA 95819, (916) 278-6437

California State University – Fresno, Department of Criminology, Fresno, CA 93740-0104, (559) 278-5715

California State University – Los Angeles, Department of Criminal Justice, Los Angeles, CA 90032, (323) 343-4618

California State University - Sacramento, Center for Delinquency/Crime Policy Studies, Sacramento, CA 95819, (916) 278-4522

California State University – San Bernardino, Department of Criminal Justice, San Bernardino, CA 92407, (909) 880-5506

Canisius College, Criminal Justice Program, Buffalo, NY 14208, (716) 888-2749

Cedarville College, Department of Criminal Justice and Public Administration, Xenia, OH 45385, (973) 766-7814

Central Arizona College, Criminal Justice Department, Coolidge, AZ 85228,
  (520) 426-4371

Central Connecticut State University, Department of Criminology, New Britain, CT
  06053, (860) 832-3139

Central Connecticut State University, Department of Criminal Justice, New Britain, CT
  06053, (860) 832-3142

Central Missouri State University, Criminal Justice Department, Warrensburg, MO
  64093, (660) 543-4950

Central Washington University, Department of Law and Justice, Ellensburg, WA 98926-
  7580, (509) 963-1779

Chadron State College, Justice Studies Department, Chadron, NE 69337,
  (308) 432-6463

Charleston Southern University, Criminal Justice Department, Charleston, SC 29423-
  8087, (843) 863-7131

Chicago State University, Department of Criminal Justice, Chicago, IL 60628,
  (773) 995-3861

Columbia College, Department of Criminal Justice, Columbia, MO 65216,
  (573) 474-8960

Columbus State University, Department of Criminal Justice, Columbus, GA 31907,
  (703) 568-2023

Concordia University – Wisconsin, Criminal Justice Department, Mequon, WI 53097,
  (414) 243-4223

Delaware Valley College, Criminal Justice Department, Doylestown, PA 18901,
  (215) 489-2214

Delta College, Criminal Justice Department, University Center, MI   48710,
  (517) 686-9110

East Carolina University, Criminal Justice Studies, Greenville, NC 27858,
  (252) 328-4190

East Tennessee State University, Department of Criminal Justice and Criminology,
  Johnson City, TN 37614, (423) 439-8662

Eastern Kentucky University, Correctional and Juvenile Justice Studies, Richmond, KY 40475-3102, (606) 622-1155

Eastern Michigan University, Department of Sociology, Anthropology and Criminology, Ypsilanti, MI 48197, (734) 487-3184

Edinboro University of Pennsylvania, Department of Political Science and Criminal Justice, Edinboro, PA 16444, (814) 732-2404

Elmira College, Sociology and Criminal Justice, Elmira, NY 14901, (607) 735-1933

Ferris State University, Criminal Justice Department, Big Rapids, MI 49307, (231) 591-5009

Florence-Darlington Technical College, Criminal Justice Department, Florence, SC 29501, (803) 661-8134

Florida Atlantic University, Criminal Justice Department, Davie, FL 33314, (954) 236-1242

Florida Gulf Coast University, Division of Criminal Justice, Fort Myers, FL 33965-6565, (941) 590-7831

Florida Metropolitan University, Department of Criminal Justice, Tampa, FL 33619, (813) 621-0041

Florida State University, School of Crime and Criminal Justice, Tallahassee, FL 32309-1127, (850) 644-7372

Florida Southern College, Department of Sociology and Criminology, Lakeland, FL 33801-5698, (813) 680-4307

Gannon University, Criminal Justice Program, University Square, Erie, PA 16541, (814) 871-7498

George Mason University, Administration of Justice, Manassas, VA 20110-2203, (703) 993-8313

George Washington University, Forensic Sciences Department, Washington, DC 20052, (202) 994-7320

Georgia State University, Department of Criminal Justice, Atlanta, GA 30302, (404) 651-3689

Grambling State University, Criminology Justice Department, Ruston, LA 71270, (318) 255-6900

Grand Valley State University, School of Criminal Justice, Allendale, MI 49401, (616) 895-2934

Green River Community College, Criminal Justice Department, Auburn, WA 98092-3699, (253) 833-9111

Governors State University, Department of Criminal Justice, University Park, IL 60466, (708) 534-4577

Illinois Central College, Criminal Justice Department, Peoria, IL 61635-0001, (309) 999-4635

Illinois State University, Department of Criminal Justice, Campus Box 5250, Normal, IL 61790-5250, (309) 438-7626

Indiana State University, Department of Criminology, 233 Holmstedt Hall, Terre Haute, IN 47809, (812) 237-2180

Indiana University, Criminal Justice Department, Bloomington, IN 48405, (812) 855-5161

Indiana University of Pennsylvania, Department of Criminology, Indiana, PA 15705, (412) 357-6244

Indiana Wesleyan University, Criminal Justice Department, Marion, IN 46953, (765) 677-2236

Jacksonville State University, Department of Criminal Justice, Jacksonville, AL 36265, (256) 782-5347

John Jay College of Criminal Justice, New York, NY 10019, (212) 237-8654

Johns Hopkins University, Baltimore, MD 21201, (410) 516-0770

Kaskaskia College, Administration of Justice, Centralia, IL 62801, (618) 545-3336

Kean University, Criminal Justice Department, Union, NJ 07083, (908) 527-2508

Kent State University, Criminal Justice Studies, 113 Bowman Hall, Kent, OH 4424-0001, (330) 672-2775

Keuka College, Criminal Justice Program, 319 Hegeman Hall, Keuka Park, NY 14478-0098, (315) 531-6830

Kutztown University, Criminal Justice Department, Kutztown, PA19530, (610) 683-4238

Lake Superior State University, Criminal Justice Department, Sault Ste Marie, MI 49783, (906) 635-2749

Langston University, Criminal Justice and Corrections Department, Langston, OK 73050, (405) 466-3345

Lewis University, Criminal Justice Department, Romeoville, IL 60446, (815) 836-5949

Long Island University, Department of Criminal Justice, Brookville, NY 11548-1300, (516) 299-2468

Long Island University – C.W. Post, Criminal Justice Department, Brookville, NY 11548, (516) 299-2592

Loyola University – Chicago, Criminal Justice Department, Chicago, IL 60611, (312) 915-7570

Lycoming College, Criminal Justice Department, Williamsport, PA 17701, (570) 321-4202

Madonna University, Criminal Justice Department, Livonia, MI 48150-1173, (734) 432-5546

Marist College, Criminal Justice Department, Poughkeepsie, NY 12601, (914) 575-3000

Marquette University, Criminal and Law Studies Program, Milwaukee, WI 53201-1881, (414) 288-5437

Marshall University, Criminal Justice Department, Huntington, WV 25755-2662, (304) 696-3083

Mercer County Community College, Criminal Justice Program, Trenton, NJ 08690, (609) 586-4800

Mercyhurst College, Criminal Justice Department, Erie, PA 16546, (814) 824-2328

Methodist College, Director of Criminal Justice Studies, Fayetteville, NC 28311, (910) 630-7050

Metropolitan State College, Department of Criminal Justice and Criminology, Denver, CO 80217-3362, (303) 556-3160

Metropolitan State University, School of Law Enforcement and Criminal Justice, St. Paul, MN 55108, (651) 649-5460

Michigan State University, School of Criminal Justice, East Lansing, MI 48824, (517) 337-1928

Middle Tennessee State University, Criminal Justice Department, Murfreesboro, TN 37132, (615) 898-5565

Minnesota State University, Department of Sociology and Corrections, 113 Armstrong Hall, Mankato, IL 56001, (507) 389-5612

Minnesota State University – Mankato, Political Science and Law Enforcement, Morris Hall 109, Mankato, MN 56001, (507) 389-1018

Minot State University, Department of Criminal Justice, Minot, ND 58707, (701) 858-3140

Mississippi Valley State University, Department of Criminal Justice, Itta Bena, MS 38941, (662) 254-3641

Missouri Valley College, Criminal Justice Department, Marshall, MO 65340-3407, (660) 831-4179

Mitchell College, Criminal Justice Department, New London, CT 06320, (860) 701-5000

Monmouth University, Criminal Justice Department, Withey Hall, West Long Branch, NJ 07764, (732) 571-3600

Morehead State University, Sociology, Social Work, and Criminology, Morehead, KY, 40351, (606) 783-2551

Mount Marty College, Criminal Justice Studies, Yankton, SD 57078, (605) 668-1465

Murray State University, Department of Criminal Justice, Murray, KY 42071, (502) 762-2700

New Hampshire Technical Institute, Criminal Justice Department, Concord, NH 03301-7412, (603) 271-6952

New Jersey City University, Department of Criminal Justice, Jersey City, NJ 07305, (201) 200-3492

New Mexico State University, Department of Criminal Justice, Las Cruces, NM 88003-0001, (505) 646-5376

Niagara University, Department of Criminal Justice, Niagara University, NY 14109-1941, (716) 286-8081

North Carolina Central University, Department of Criminal Justice, Durham, NC 27707, (919) 530-2010

North Carolina Justice Academy, Drawer 99, Salemburg, NC 28385, (910) 525-4151

North Georgia College State University, Department of Political Science and Criminal Justice, Dahlonega, GA 30597, (706) 864-1908

Northeastern State University, Department of Criminal Justice, Tahlequah, OK 74464, (918) 456-5511

Northeastern University, College of Criminal Justice, Boston, MA 02115, (617) 373-3362

Northern Arizona University, Criminal Justice Department, Flagstaff, AZ 86011-5055, (520) 523-6528

Northern Kentucky University, School of Law, Highland Heights, KY 41099, (606) 572-5253

Northern Michigan University, Criminal Justice Department, Marquette, MI 49855, (906) 227-2660

Northwest State University, Criminal Justice Department, Deridder, LA 70634, (318) 462-1197

Norwich University, Justice Studies Department, Northfield, VT 05663, (802) 485-2368

Old Dominion University, Department of Sociology and Criminal Justice, Norfolk, VA 23529, (757) 683-5931

Park College, Criminal Justice Department, Parkville, MO 64152, (816) 741-2000

Pennsylvania State Atloona, Criminal Justice Program, Atloona, PA 16601-3760, (814) 949-5507

Pennsylvania State University, Crime, Law, and Justice Program, Department of Sociology, University Park, PA 16802-6207, (814) 863-0275

Pima College East, Justice Studies Program, Tucson, AZ 85709-4000, (520) 206-7865

Portland State University, Division of Administration of Justice, Portland, OR 97207, (503) 725-8090

Radford University, Department of Criminal Justice, Radford, VA 24142, (540) 831-6148

Ramapo College – New Jersey, Criminal Justice Department, Montvale, NJ 07645, (201) 476-0401

Richard Stockton College of New Jersey, Department of Criminal Justice, College Drive, Pomona, NJ 08057, (609) 652-4625

Rio Salado College, Law Enforcement Programs, Tempe, AZ 85281-6950, (480) 517-8257

Rochester Institute of Technology, Department of Criminal Justice, Rochester, NY 14623, (518) 442-5631

Roger Williams University, School of Justice Studies, Bristol, RI 02806, (401) 254-3394

Rowan University, Law & Justice Studies, Glassboro, NJ 08028, (856) 256-4399

Rutgers University, School of Criminal Justice, Newark, NJ 07102, (973) 353-5073

Saginaw Valley State College, Criminal Justice Department, University Center, MI 48710, (517) 790-4078

Saint Ambrose University, Criminal Justice Department, Davenport, IA 52803, (319) 333-6157

Saint Cloud State University, Criminal Justice Department, St. Cloud, MN 56301-4498, (320) 255-3974

Saint Leo College, Criminology Department, St. Leo, FL 33574-6665, (352) 588-8402

Saint Louis University, Department of Sociology and Criminal Justice, St. Louis, MO 63103, (314) 977-2895

Saint Xavier University, Criminal Justice Dept., Chicago, IL 60657-4845, (773) 298-3162

Salem State College, Department of Criminal Justice, Carlisle, MA 01741, (978) 542-6748

Sam Houston State University, College of Criminal Justice, Huntsville, TX 77341-2296, (409) 294-1637

San Jacinto College North, Criminal Justice Department, Houston, TX 77049-4513, (281) 458-4050

San Jose State University, Administration of Justice Department, San Jose, CA 95192, (408) 924-2940

Seattle University, Department of Criminal Justice, Seattle, WA 98122, (206) 296-5478

Seton Hall University, Department of Criminal Justice, South Orange, NJ 07079, (973) 275-5885

Shippensburg University, Criminal Justice Department, Shippensburg, PA 17257, (717) 477-1770

Simpson College, Criminal Justice Department, Indianola, IA 50125, (515) 961-1583

Snow College, Criminal Justice, Ephraim, UT 84627-1203, (801) 283-4021

Sonoma State University, Department of Criminal Justice, Rohnert Park, CA 94928, (707) 664-3962

South Carolina State University, Criminal Justice Program, Orangeburg, SC 29117-0001, (803) 536-8791/8600

Southeast Missouri State University, Department of Criminal Justice, Cape Girardeau, MO 63701, (573) 651-2541

Southeastern Louisiana University, Department of Sociology, Criminal Justice, and Social Work, 260 D. Vickers Hall, Hammond, LA 70402, (504) 549-2110

Southern Illinois University – Carbondale, Center for the Study of Crime, Carbondale, IL 62901-4504, (618) 453-6371

Southern Oregon University, Department of Criminology, Ashland, OR 97520-5081, (541) 552-6507

Southern University, Department of Sociology and Criminal Justice, Baton Rouge, LA 10051, (504) 771-2011

Southwestern Adventist University, Criminal Justice Department, Keene, TX 76059, (817) 556-4732

State University of New York, School of Criminal Justice, Albany, NY 12222, (518) 442-5317

State University of New York – Brockport, Department of Criminal Justice, Brockport, NY 14420, (716) 395-5501

State University of West Georgia, Department of Sociology, Anthropology, and Criminology, Carrollton, GA 30118, (770) 577-3920

Stephen F. Austin State University, Department of Criminal Justice, Nacogdoches, TX 75962-3064, (409) 468-4408

Sul Ross State University, Criminal Justice Department, Alpine, TX 79832, (915) 837-8166

SUNY College of Brockport, Brockport, NY 14420, (716) 395-2524

Tarleton State University, Criminal Justice Department, Stephenville, TX 76402, (254) 968-9024

Taylor University, Justice Education Department, Ft. Wayne, IN 46807, (219) 456-2111

Teikyo Post University, Criminal Justice Program, Waterbury, CT 06723-2540, (203) 596-4667

Tennessee State University, Department of Criminal Justice, Nashville, TN 37209, (615) 963-5032

Temple University, Crime and Justice Research Institute, Havertown, PA 19083, (610) 789-0908

Texas A & M University – Commerce, Department of Sociology and Criminal Justice, Commerce, TX 75429, (903) 886-5331

Texas A & M University – Corpus Christi, Criminal Justice Department, Corpus Christi, TX 78412, (512) 994-2697

Texas State University – San Marcos, Criminal Justice Department, San Marcos, TX 78666-4616, (512) 245-2174

The Citadel, Department of Political Science and Criminal Justice, Charleston, SC 29409, (843) 953-6786

The College of New Jersey, Department of Law & Justice, Ewing, NJ 08628-0718, (609) 771-2271

Tiffin University, School of Criminal Justice, Tiffin, OH 44883, (800) 968-6446

Truman State University, Justice Systems Program, Kirksville, MO 63501-4221, (660) 785-4667

Tulane University – University College, Criminal Justice Program, New Orleans, LA 70118, (504) 283-4196

University of Alabama, Criminal Justice Department, Tuscaloosa, AL 35487-0320, (205) 553-6885

University of Alabama - Birmingham, Department of Justice Sciences, Birmingham, AL 35294-2060

University of Alaska-Anchorage, Justice Center, Anchorage, AK 99508, (907) 786-1810

University of Albany, School of Criminal Justice, Albany, NY 12222, (518) 442-5224

University of Arkansas – Little Rock, Criminal Justice Department, Little Rock, AR 72204, (501) 569-3195

University of Buffalo, Regional Community Policing Center, Buffalo, NY 14214-3003, (716) 829-3520

University of California – Irvine, Department of Criminology, Law and Society, Irvine, CA 92697-7080, (714) 824-1437

University of Central Florida, Department of Criminal Justice and Legal Studies, Orlando, FL 32816-1600, (407) 823-5944

University of Central Florida – Daytona Beach, Daytona Beach, FL 32120, (904) 255-7423

University of Central Oklahoma, Department of Sociology and Criminal Justice, Edmond, OK 73034-5209, (405) 974-5626

University of Cincinnati, Center for Criminal Justice Research, Cincinnati, OH 45221-0389, (513) 558-0857

University of Colorado – Denver, Department of Criminal Justice, Denver, CO 80217-3364, (303) 556-5995

University of Dayton, Criminal Justice Studies Program, Dayton, OH, (937) 229-4242

University of Florida, Criminology and Law, Gainesville, FL 32611, (352) 392-1025

University of Great Falls, Criminal Justice Department, Bozeman, MT 59715, (406) 587-9474

University of Houston – Downtown, Department of Criminal Justice, Houston, TX 77002-1001, (713) 221-8016

University of Idaho, Department of Sociology and Justice Studies, Moscow, ID 83844, (208) 885-6117

University of Illinois – Chicago, Department of Criminal Justice, Chicago, IL 60607-7140, (312) 355-2469

University of Illinois – Springfield, Criminal Justice Department, Springfield, IL 19243, (217) 786-7586

University of Illinois – Urbana, Police Training Institute, Champaign, IL 61820, (217) 333-7826

University of Louisiana – Lafayette, Criminal Justice Department, Lafayette, LA 70504, (337) 482-6180

University of Louisville, Justice Administration Department, Louisville, KY 40292, (502) 852-0326

University of Maine, Sociology and Criminal Justice Department, Presque Isle, ME 04769, (207) 768-9465

University of Maryland, Department of Criminology, 2220 LeFrak Hall, College Park, MD 20742, (301) 405-4699

University of Massachusetts – Boston, Criminal Justice Program, Boston, MA 02125-3393, (617) 287-6260

University of Massachusetts – Lowell, Department of Criminal Justice, Lowell, MA 01854-3044, (508) 934-4262

University of Memphis, Department of Criminology and Criminal Justice, 405 Mitchell Hall, Memphis, TN 38152,(901) 678-8155

University of Missouri - Kansas City, Department of Sociology, Criminal Justice, Criminology, Kansas City, MO 64110, (816) 235-5706

University of Missouri – St. Louis, Department of Criminology and Criminal Justice, Bonne Terre, MO 63628, (314) 516-5031

University of Nebraska – Kearney, Department of Criminal Justice, Kearney, NE 68849, (308) 865-8510

University of Nebraska - Omaha, Department of Criminal Justice, Omaha, NE 68182, (402) 554-3945

University of Nevada, Criminal Justice Department, Las Vegas, NV 89154-5009, (702) 895-0246

University of Nevada – Reno, Department of Criminal Justice, Reno, NV 89557, (775) 784-6164

University of New Haven, Department of Criminal Justice, West Haven, CT 06516, (203) 932-7376

University of North Carolina, Department of Criminal Justice, Charlotte, NC 28223-0001, (704) 547-2009

University of North Carolina - Charlotte, Department of Criminal Justice, Charlotte, NC 28223, (704) 547-2510

University of North Carolina – Pembroke, Criminal Justice Department, Pembroke, NC 28358, (910) 521-7582

University of North Dakota, Criminal Justice Studies, Grand Forks, ND 58202, (701) 777-4181

University of North Texas, Department of Criminal Justice, Denton, TX 76203-5130, (940) 565-4591

University of Northern Iowa, Department of Sociology, Anthropology and Criminal Justice, Cedar Falls, IA 50614, (319) 273-2786

University of Saint Thomas, Sociology and Criminal Justice Department, St. Paul, MN 55105, (651) 962-5631

University of Scranton, Department of Sociology and Criminal Justice, Scranton, PA 18510-4605, (570) 941-7476

University of South Alabama, Department of Political Science and Criminal Justice, Humanities Building, # 226, Mobile AL 36688-0002, (334) 460-7095

University of South Carolina, College of Criminal Justice, Columbia, SC, (803) 777-6424

University of South Carolina – Spartanburg, Criminal Justice Department, 800 University Way, Spartanburg, SC 29303, (865) 503-5606

University of South Dakota, Criminal Justice Studies, Vermillion, SD 57069, (605) 677-5242

University of South Florida, Department of Criminology, Tampa, FL 33815, (813) 974-9708

University of Southern California, Center of Administration of Justice, Tyler Building Room 108, Los Angeles, CA 90007, (714) 278-2795

University of Tennessee – Chattanooga, Criminal Justice Department, Chattanooga, TN 37403, (423) 875-2166

University of Texas - Arlington, Criminal Justice Department, Ft. Worth, TX 76111, (817) 816-4037

University of Texas – Brownsville, Criminal Justice Department, Brownsville, TX 78520, (956) 983-7407

University of Texas – El Paso, Criminal Justice Program, Vowell Hall, El Paso, TX 79968, (915) 747-7943

University of Texas – San Antonio, Division of Social, Policy Sciences, and Criminal Justice, San Antonio, TX 78249-0655, (210) 458-5605

University of West Florida, Division of Criminal Justice and Legal Studies, 11000 University Parkway, Pensacola, FL 32514-5750, (850) 474-2871

- University of Wisconsin, Criminal Justice Department, Milwaukee, WI 53201, (414) 229-2431

University of Wisconsin – Milwaukee, Criminal Justice Program, Milwaukee, WI 53201-0786, (414) 229-6038

University of Wisconsin – Parkside, Department of Criminal Justice, Kenosha, WI 53141-2000, (414) 595-3416

University of Wyoming, Department of Criminal Justice, Laramie, WY 82071-3293, (307) 766-2988

Valdosta State University, Sociology, Anthropology, and Criminal Justice, Valdosta, GA 31602-0001, (912) 333-5943

Victoria College, Criminal Justice Department, Victoria, TX 77901, (512) 572-6426

Virginia Commonwealth University, Department of Criminal Justice, Richmond, VA, (804) 828-1050

Washington State University, Criminal Justice Department, Pullman, WA 99165, (509) 332-0805

Washington State University – Spokane, Criminal Justice Program, Spokane, WA 99202-1662, (509) 358-7952

Wayne State University, Criminal Justice Department, Birmingham, MI 48202, (248) 644-4909

Weatherford College, Criminal Justice Department, Weatherford, TX 76086, (817) 598-6313

Weber State University, Criminal Justice Department, Ogden, UT 84408-1206, (801) 626-6151

West Chester University, West Chester, PA 19382, (610) 436-2630

West Liberty State College, Criminal Justice Department, Wheeling, WV 26003, (304) 232-2839

West Virginia State College, Criminal Justice Department, Institute, WV 25112-1000, (304) 766-3082

Western Carolina University, Department of Criminal Justice, Cullowhee, NC 28723, (828) 227-2173

Western Connecticut State University, Division of Justice and Law Administration, Danbury, CT 06810, (837-8514

Western Illinois University, Department of Law Enforcement, One University Circle, Macomb, IL 61455, (309) 298-2251

Westfield State College, Criminal Justice Department, Westfield, MA 01086, (413) 572-5761

Wheeling Jesuit University, Department of Criminal Justice, Wheeling, WV 26003-6243, (304) 243-2567

Wichita State University, Regional Community Policing Institute, Wichita, KS 67260-0135, (316) 978-5896

Widener University, Criminal Justice and Social Science Division, Chester, PA 19013, (610) 499-4525

Winona State University, Department of Sociology and Criminal Justice, Winona, MN 55987, (507) 457-5670

Xavier University, Criminal Justice Department, Cohen Center, Cincinnati, OH 45207-7371, (513) 745-3518

Youngstown State University, Criminal Justice Department, One University Plaza, Youngstown, OH 44555, (330) 742-3279

GRADUATE EDUCATION

Law school and graduate school work in a variety of disciplines that are excellent options for the criminal justice majors. It is important to possess career goals in mind before considering a specific graduate program. Criminal justice majors may be interested in graduate degrees in criminal justice, public administration, business administration, social work, psychology, sociology, among others. Once you know what area you want to pursue, you should examine the attached graduate directories to decide which schools will meet your needs in terms of program, academic requirements, cost and geographical location.

A criminal justice faculty and/or pre-law advisor can help in evaluating your potential for such endeavors, in selecting an appropriate school and in providing you with letters of recommendation.

THE FOLLOWING COLLEGES/UNIVERSITIES OFFER THE M.A. OR M.S IN CRIMINAL JUSTICE

ALABAMA

Auburn University, Public Safety Dept., Montgomery, AL 36117, (205) 244-3691

Jacksonville St. Univ., College of CJ, Jacksonville, AL 36265, (205) 782-5335

University of Alabama, CJ Dept., Tuscaloosa, AL 35487, (205) 348-7795

University of Alabama, CJ Dept., Birmingham, AL 35294, (205) 934-2069

ALASKA

University of Alaska, Justice Ctr., Anchorage, AK 99508, (907) 786- 4608

ARIZONA

Arizona St. Univ., School of Justice Studies, Tempe, AZ 85287, (602) 965-7684

Northern Arizona Univ., Sociology, SW & CJ Dept., Flagstaff, AZ 86011, (602) 523-1520

ARKANSAS

Univ. of Arkansas, CJ Dept., Little Rock, AR 72204, (501) 569-3195

CALIFORNIA

California St. Univ., CJ Division, Sacramento, CA 95819, (916) 278-6487

California St. Univ., CJ Dept, San Bernardino, CA 92407, (714) 880-5506

Claremont Grad. School, Center for Politics & Policy, Claremont, CA 91711, (714) 621-1148

San Jose St. Univ., AOJ Dept., San Jose, CA 95192, (408) 924-2940

Univ. of California - Berkeley, Sociology Dept., Berkeley, CA 94720

Univ. of California - Irvine, Program in Social Ecology, Irvine, CA 92717

CONNECTICUT

University of New Haven, Public Mgt. & Forensic Science Program, West Haven, CT 06516, (203) 932-7116

DELAWARE

Univ. of Delaware, Sociology & CJ Dept., Newark, DE 19716, (302) 451-2581

DISTRICT OF COLUMBIA

George Washington Univ., CJ Dept., Washington, DC, 20052, (202) 994-7319

FLORIDA

Florida International University, CJ Dept., North Miami, FL 33181, (305) 940-5850

Florida St. University, School of Criminology, Tallahassee, FL 32306, (904) 644-4050

University of South Florida, Criminology Dept., Tampa, FL 33620, (813) 974- 2815

GEORGIA

Albany State College, CJ Dept., Albany, GA 31705, (912) 430-4864

Georgia State University, CJ Dept., Atlanta, GA 30303, (404) 651-3515

Valdosta State College, Sociology, Anthropology, & CJ Dept., Valdosta, GA 31698, (912) 333-5943

ILLINOIS

Illinois State University, CJ Dept., Normal, IL 61761, (309) 438-7626

South Illinois University, Administration of Justice Dept., Carbondale, IL 62901, (618) 453-5701

University of Illinois, CJ Dept., Chicago, IL 60680, (312) 996-5262

Western Illinois University, Law Enforcement Dept., Macomb, IL 61455, (309) 298-1038

INDIANA

Indiana St Univ., Criminology Dept., Terre Haute, IN 47809, (812) 237-2190

Indiana University, CJ Dept., Bloomington, IN 47405, (812) 855-9880

Indiana University Northwest, School of Public & Environmental Affairs, Gary, IN 46408, (219) 980-6605

KANSAS

Wichita State Univ., AOJ Dept., Wichita, KS 67208, (316) 689-3710

KENTUCKY

Eastern Kentucky University, School of Law Enforcement, Richmond, KY 40475, (606) 622-3565

University of Louisville, School of Justice Administration, Louisville, KY 40292, (502) 588-6567

LOUISIANA

Grambling St. Univ., CJ Dept., Grambling, LA 71245, (318) 274-2746

Northeast LA Univ., CJ Dept., Monroe, LA 71209, (318) 342-4026

Southern University, Dept. of Social Sciences, New Orleans, LA 70126 (504) 286-5000

MARYLAND

University of Maryland, Institute of CJ and Criminology, College Park, MD 20742 (301) 405-4703

MASSACHUSETTS

Northeastern University, College of Criminal Justice, Boston, MA 02115, (617) 437-3327

Westfield State College, CJ Dept., Westfield, MA 01086, (413) 568-3311

Univ. of MA at Lowell, CJ Dept., Lowell, MA 01854, (508) 934-4246

MICHIGAN

Eastern Michigan Univ., Soc., Anthro. & Criminology Dept., Ypsilanti, MI 48197, (313) 487-0012

Michigan St. Univ., School of Criminal Justice, East Lansing, MI 48824, (517) 355-2192

Wayne State University, CJ Program, Detroit, MI 48202, (313) 577- 2705

Western Michigan Univ., Sociology, Anthropology & Criminology Dept., Kalamazoo, MI 49008, (616) 387-5281

MINNESOTA

St. Cloud University, CJ Dept., St. Cloud, MN 56301, (612) 255-4101

MISSISSIPPI

University of Southern Mississippi, CJ Dept., Hattiesburg, MS 39406, (601) 266-4509

MISSOURI

University of Missouri, Sociology/AJ Dept., Kansas City, MO 64110, (816) 276-1597

NEBRASKA

University of Nebraska, CJ Dept., Omaha, NE 68182, (402) 554-2610

NEW JERSEY

Rowan University, Criminal Justice, Glassboro, NJ 08028, (856) 256-4399

Rutgers University, School of Criminal Justice, Newark, NJ 07102, (201) 648-5870

NEW MEXICO

New Mexico St. Univ., CJ Dept., Las Cruces, NM 88003, (505) 646-3316

NEW YORK

John Jay College of Criminal Justice, CJ Dept., City University of New York, New York, NY 10019, (212) 237-8695

State University of New York, School of Criminal Justice, Albany, NY 12222, (518) 442- 5210

State University of New York, CJ Dept., Buffalo, NY 14222, (716) 878- 6819

NORTH CAROLINA

North Carolina Central University, CJ Dept., Durham, NC 27707, (919) 560-6280

University of North Carolina, CJ Dept., Charlotte, NC 28223, (704) 547-4776

OHIO

Kent State University, CJ Dept., Kent, OH 44242, (216) 672-2775

University of Cincinnati, CJ Dept., Cincinnati, OH 45221, (513) 556- 5827

Youngstown State University, CJ Dept., Youngstown, OH 44555, (216) 742- 3279

OKLAHOMA

Univ. of Central Oklahoma, Sociology & CJ Dept., Edmond, OK 73034, (405) 341-2980

Oklahoma City University, CJ Dept., Oklahoma City, OK 73106, (405) 521-5045

Oklahoma State University, Sociology Dept., Stillwater, OK 74078, (405) 744-6105

OREGON

Portland State University, AOJ Dept., Portland, OR 97207, (503) 725- 4014

PENNSYLVANIA

Indiana University of PA, Criminology Dept., Indiana, PA 15705, (412) 357-2720

Mercyhurst College, CJ Dept., Erie, PA 16546, (814) 824-2266

Penn. St. University, AOJ Program, University Park, PA 16802, (814) 863-0078

St. Joseph's University, Sociology & CJ Dept., Philadelphia, PA 19131

SOUTH CAROLINA

University of South Carolina, College of Criminal Justice, Columbia, SC 29208, (803) 777-7097

TENNESSEE

East Tennessee St. University, CJ and Criminology Dept., Johnson City, TN 37614, (615) 929-6807

Univ. of Memphis, CJ Dept., Memphis, TN 38152, (901) 678-2737

Middle Tennessee St. University, CJ Dept., Murfreesboro, TN 37132, (615) 755-4135

University of Tennessee, CJ Dept., Chattanooga, TN 37403, (615) 755-4135

TEXAS

Sam Houston State Univ., College of Criminal Justice, Huntsville, TX 77341, (409) 294-1631

Texas St. Univ. – San Marcos, CJ Dept., San Marcos, TX 78666, (512) 245-2174

University of Texas at Arlington, CJ Dept., Arlington, TX 76019, (817) 273-3318

VIRGINIA

Virginia Commonwealth Univ., Justice & Risk Mgt. Dept., Richmond, VA 23284, (804) 367-1050

WASHINGTON

Washington State University, Program in CJ, Pullman, WA 99164, (509) 335-2544

Washington State University, CJ Program, Spokane, WA 99204, (509) 456-3275

WEST VIRGINIA

Marshall University, CJ Dept., Huntington, WV 25755, (304) 696-3196

WISCONSIN

Marquette University, Criminology & Law Dept., Milwaukee, WI 53233, (414) 288-6838

University of Wisconsin, CJ Dept., Milwaukee, WI 53201, (414) 229-6030

THE FOLLOWING UNIVERSITIES OFFER THE Ph.D. IN CRIMINAL JUSTICE

Arizona State University, School of Justice Studies, Tempe, AZ 85287,
602-965-7684

Sam Houston St. University, College of Criminal Justice, Huntsville, TX 77341,
409-294-1631

Claremont Graduate School, Center for Politics & Policy, Claremont, CA 91711,
714-521-1148

State University of NY- Albany, School of Criminal Justice, Albany, NY 12222,
518-442-5210

Florida State University, School of Criminology, Tallahassee, FL 32306,
904-644-4050

Univ. of California-Irvine, Program in Social Ecology, Irvine, CA 92717,
714-856-6094

Indiana University, Dept. of CJ, Bloomington, IN 47405,
812-855-9325

Indiana Univ. of Pennsylvania, Dept. of Criminology, Indiana, PA 15705,
412-357-2720

University of Cincinnati, Dept. of Criminal Justice, Cincinnati, OH 45221,
513-556-5827

John Jay College of CJ, 444 West 56th St., New York, NY 10019,
212-237-8695

University of Delaware, Dept. of Sociology & CJ, Newark, DE 19716,
302-451-2581

Michigan State Univ., School of CJ, East Lansing, MI 48824,
517-355-2192

University of Nebraska, CJ Dept., Omaha, NE 68182,
402-554-2610

University of Maryland, Dept. of Criminology and CJ, College Park, MD 20742,
301-405-4703

Penn. State Univ., Sociology/AOJ Dept., University Park, PA 16802, 814-863-0078

Univ. of Missouri-St. Louis, Dept. of Crim./CJ, St. Louis, MO 63121, 314-553-5031

Portland State University, CJ Program, Portland, OR 97207, 503-229-4014

Rutgers University, School of CJ, Newark, NJ 07102, 201-648-5870

Temple University, CJ Dept., Philadelphia, PA 19122, 215-204-7918[15]

CHAPTER TEN

CONCLUSION

CHAPTER TEN: CONCLUSION

No matter how well prepared you are for the internship, seeking an internship is difficult. You must be extremely patient, especially when you are pursuing state and federal governmental internships. You will have to wait for responses to initial inquiries, interviews and final decisions.

As you move along your career path, be aware that the assessment of your personal needs, your skills and your geographical limitations may change as you gain experience and as your personal situation changes. You should periodically assess your career to determine if your personal needs are being met.

The most important aspect of the internship selection is that you must be able to live with yourself and with the daily issues of justice, fairness and punishment. You must always examine your values and the behavior you exhibit in the workplace. It may be difficult to complete a criminal justice internship because of the internal complex legalities, peer pressure and observing individuals functioning at their worst. If you possess the attitude, philosophy and personal drive of coping with the myriad emotions and frustrations inherent in this field, then a criminal justice career can be very rewarding in terms of the assistance you will provide to fellow citizens in need.

In deciding which internship is best suited for you and your needs, you must consider educational requirements, background limitations and experience requirements.

Finally, internships are an excellent way to discover if a specific area of criminal justice is a good fit for you. An internship is an opportunity to receive supervised, practical on-the-job training in specific areas of the criminal justice system.

We encourage you to pursue the internship with the best wishes and may the completion of the internship coincide with your future endeavors.

APPENDIX A

INTERNSHIP APPLICATION

Please fully complete the following information and write legibly.

Full Name:_____Social Security #:_____

School:_____Date of Graduation:_____

Major:_____Minor:_____

Current status: college junior_____   college senior_____   graduate student_____

Would you receive course credit for this internship?_____If so, state _____
credits.

Current phone number:_____

Current
address:_____
                  street   city, state   zip code

Permanent phone number:_____

Permanent
address:_____
                  street   city, state   zip code

Name of faculty/coordinator of internship:_____

Special skills or equipment that you are familiar with:_____

_____

_____

Departments of interest (see Internship Opportunities):_____

_____

_____

Which semester are you applying for: Winter_____   Spring_____   Summer_____
Fall_____

Start date:_____   Ending date:_____

Total number of hours available to work each week: (Maximum 40 hours, five days/week)

Mon._____   Tues._____   Wed._____   Thurs._____   Fri._____   Sat._____
Sun._____

APPENDIX B

AGENCY
BACKGROUND INVESTIGATION FORM

Misrepresentation or misstatement of fact is sufficient cause for the rejection of an applicant or removal from the position._____APPLICANT INITIAL

NAME:_____

ADDRESS:_____

CITY:_____STATE:_____ZIP CODE:_____

ALIAS/NICKNAMES:_____

MAIDEN NAME OR NAME CHANGE:_____

DATE OF BIRTH:_____SS#:_____

TELEPHONE NUMBER: (H):_____
(Include area code)
                                                     (W):_____

E-MAIL ADDRESS:_____

MARKS/SCARS/TATTOOS:_____

APPENDIX C

INTERNSHIP AGREEMENT

Between

_____ Department of _____ University or College and

Agency_____.

The _____ Department of _____ University designates _____ (agency) as an approved internship placement providing a rich blend of practical laboratory experiences yielded by the criminal justice agency or related agency.

The _____ Department and the _____ Agency commit themselves to cooperative efforts as described below, in provision of supervised educational internship experiences for the _____ Department.

This agreement becomes effective on _____, remains in force for a period _____ of _____ year(s), and renews itself annually, unless either the _____ Department or the _____ Agency indicates a need for a review or change.

Any adjustments to the agreement will be included in a written addendum.

In the event of unforeseen circumstances which significantly affect the student's educational plan, each party with inform the other in writing, so that the appropriate changes in their agreement may be made within a reasonable amount of time (14 days), to assure sufficient time for planning.

The _____ Department Agrees To:

1. Work cooperatively with the agency in designing appropriate learning experiences and to actively participate with the student and the Internship Supervisor or Agency site manager in the decision-making concerning the educational appropriateness, timing and the reasonableness of the internship experiences.

2. Respect the autonomy of the agency to set its own program as a service delivery system.

3. Interview, screen, select and recommend students to be placed at the agency, and to make alternate plans for placement of student(s) in the event that such planning becomes necessary.

4. Formulate and execute all educational decisions concerning the student, such as: grades, credits, hours completed within the agency and the curriculum in general.

5. Provide consultation to appropriate staff of the agency in the general development of its internship program.

6. The faculty/coordinator of the Internship Program will serve as the Internship Consultant to the agency who will:

   a. Serve as the principal liaison between the department and the agency during each academic semester.

   b. Be available for the agency as need may be concerning the relationships between the agency and the department.

   c. Make periodic visits to the agency to review the student(s) progress.

   d. Discuss policies and procedures of the Internship Course.

7. Provide opportunities for appropriate evaluations of the agency as a setting of student learning.

8. Provide a copy of the department's course syllabus.

The Agency Agrees To:

1. Accept the policy of the department that students are assigned in accordance with the provisions of the Federal Civil Rights Act.

2. Adhere to the objectives of the department as contained in its course syllabus.

3. Accept the conditions stipulated in the course syllabus.

4. Involve the students in meaningful agency programs by utilizing appropriate assignments or tasks.

5. Allow students to use their work product for academic discussion with the Faculty/Coordinator of the Internship Program.

6. Assure that each supervisor or site manager or designated representative will have adequate time within his/her work schedule to:

   a. Satisfy the educational objectives of the students through development of learning opportunities.

b. Prepare for regularly scheduled conferences with students.

c. Meet with the Faculty/Coordinator of the Internship Program at periodic intervals to discuss learning opportunities and student performance.

d. Prepare reports and evaluation as required by the department.

e. Attend appropriate department sponsored meetings or conferences.

7. Permit the use of facilities by students of the department during the period of the placement, including:

a. Space for students in an area sufficiently private for carrying on the assigned work or activity.

b. Clerical services for those records and reports which are produced for the agency.

c. Access to client and agency records as it relates to agency supervision.

8. Assure that the Faculty/Coordinator of the Internship Program is advised of policy and service changes and developments which may affect student learning or the department's curriculum.

9. Inform the Faculty/Coordinator of any early or immediate problems that may develop concerning a student's progress or performance.

10. Provide reimbursement of all student travel expenses on agency business.

11. Observe the University/College calendar with respect to student holiday and vacation periods.

12. Adhere to course objectives:

a. _____

b. _____

c. _____

d. _____

e. _____

FOR THE AGENCY: FOR THE:

_____   UNIVERSITY OR COLLEGE

_____   DEPARTMENT

BY:_____   BY:_____

                                         FACULTY/COORDINATOR

                                         OF INTERNSHIP PROGRAM

DATE:_____   DATE:_____

APPENDIX D

WAIVER AND RELEASE AGREEMENT
TO INTERNSHIP COORDINATOR

I, _____ , am a student at _____ University or
_____College, and have agreed to participate in the _____
Department Criminal Justice Internship Program from _____ until _____.
In consideration for being permitted to participate in the program, I hereby agree and
represent that:

1. I have or will secure health insurance to provide adequate coverage for any
   injuries or illnesses that I may sustain or experience while participating in
   the program. By my signature below I certify that I have confirmed that my
   health care coverage will adequately cover me during the duration of the
   program, and hereby release the State of _____, _____
   University or _____ College, and the employees and agents of
   either, from any responsibility or liability for expenses incurred by me for
   injuries or illnesses (including death) that I may experience during the
   program.

2. I agree to conduct myself during the program in conformance with course
   requirements within the syllabus and with policies established by the
   University or College and agree to be under the authority and supervision of
   the Internship Coordinator/Faculty member or other University or College
   approved and designated supervisor.

3. I understand that the University or College reserves the right to decline to
   retain me in the program at any time should my actions or general behavior,
   in the sole discretion of the University or College, be determined to impede
   or obstruct the progress of the program in any way.

4. I understand that, although the University or College has made every
   reasonable effort to assure my safety while participating in the program, that
   there are unavoidable risks in travel and other activities that I will undertake
   as part of my participation in the program, and I hereby release and promise
   not to sue the State of _____, _____University or
   _____ College, or the employees and agents of either, for any
   damages or injury (including death) caused by, deriving from, or associated
   with my participation in the program, except for such damages or injury as
   may be caused by the gross negligence or willful misconduct of the
   employees or agents of the University or College.

5. I agree that, should any provision or aspect of this agreement be found to be unenforceable, that all remaining provisions of the agreement will remain in full force and effect.

6. I represent that my agreement to the provisions herein is wholly voluntary, and further understand that, prior to signing this agreement, I have the right to consult with the Advisor, Counselor, or Attorney of my choice.

7. I agree that, should there be any dispute concerning my participation in the program that would require the adjudication of a court of law, such adjudication will occur in the court of, and be determined by the laws of, the State of _____.

8. I represent that I am at least eighteen years of age or, if not, that I have secured below the signature of my parent or guardian as well as my own.

Dated: _____   _____
                                          Signature

                                          _____
                                          Name (please print)

Dated: _____   _____
                                          Signature of Parent or Guardian

                                          _____
                                          Name of Parent or
                                          Guardian (please print)

APPENDIX E

WAIVER AND RELEASE AGREEMENT
TO AGENCY

I, _____, am a student at _____ University or
_____College, and have agreed to participate in the _____
Department Criminal Justice Internship Program from _____ until _____.
In consideration for being permitted to participate in the program; I hereby agree and
represent that:

1. I have or will secure health insurance to provide adequate coverage for any
    injuries or illnesses that I may sustain or experience while participating in
    the program. By my signature below I certify that I have confirmed that my
    health care coverage will adequately cover me during the duration of the
    program, and hereby release the State of _____, _____
    University or _____ College, and the employees and agents of
    either, from any responsibility or liability for expenses incurred by me for
    injuries or illnesses (including death) that I may experience during the
    program.

2. I agree to conduct myself during the program in conformance with course
    requirements within the syllabus and with policies established by the
    University or College and agree to be under the authority and supervision of
    the Internship Coordinator/Faculty member or other University or College
    approved and designated supervisor.

3. I understand that the University or College reserves the right to decline to
    retain me in the program at any time should my actions or general behavior,
    in the sole discretion of the University or College, be determined to impede
    or obstruct the progress of the program in any way.

4. I understand that, although the University or College has made every
    reasonable effort to assure my safety while participating in the program, that
    there are unavoidable risks in travel and other activities that I will undertake
    as part of my participation in the program, and I hereby release and promise
    not to sue the State of _____, _____University or
    _____ College, or the employees and agents of either, for any
    damages or injury (including death) caused by, deriving from, or associated
    with my participation in the program, except for such damages or injury as
    may be caused by the gross negligence or willful misconduct of the
    employees or agents of the University or College.

5. I agree that, should any provision or aspect of this agreement be found to be
    unenforceable, that all remaining provisions of the agreement will remain in
    full force and effect.

6. I represent that my agreement to the provisions herein is wholly voluntary, and further understand that, prior to signing this agreement, I have the right to consult with the Advisor, Counselor, or Attorney of my choice.

7. I agree that, should there be any dispute concerning my participation in the program that would require the adjudication of a court of law, such adjudication will occur in the court of, and be determined by the laws of, the State of _____.

8. I represent that I am at least eighteen years of age or, if not, that I have secured below the signature of my parent or guardian as well as my own.

Dated: _____   _____
                                    Signature

                                    _____
                                    Name (please print)

Dated: _____   _____
                                    Signature of Parent or Guardian

                                    _____
                                    Name of Parent or
                                    Guardian (please print)

APPENDIX F

INTERNSHIP AGREEMENT

Between

_____ Department of _____ University or College and

Agency_____.

The _____ Department of _____ University designates
_____ (agency) as an approved internship placement providing a rich blend of practical laboratory experiences yielded by the criminal justice agency or related agency.

The _____ Department and the _____ Agency commit themselves to cooperative efforts as described below, in provision of supervised educational internship experiences for the _____ Department.

This agreement becomes effective on _____, remains in force for a period _____ of _____ year(s), and renews itself annually, unless either the _____ Department or the _____ Agency indicates a need for a review or change.

Any adjustments to the agreement will be included in a written addendum.

In the event of unforeseen circumstances which significantly affect the student's educational plan, each party with inform the other in writing, so that the appropriate changes in their agreement may be made within a reasonable amount of time (14 days), to assure sufficient time for planning.

The _____ Department Agrees To:

1. Work cooperatively with the agency in designing appropriate learning experiences and to actively participate with the student and the Internship Supervisor or Agency site manager in the decision-making concerning the educational appropriateness, timing and the reasonableness of the internship experiences.

2. Respect the autonomy of the agency to set its own program as a service delivery system.

3. Interview, screen, select and recommend students to be placed at the agency, and to make alternate plans for placement of student(s) in the event that such planning becomes necessary.

4. Formulate and execute all educational decisions concerning the student, such as: grades, credits, hours completed within the agency and the curriculum in general.

5. Provide consultation to appropriate staff of the agency in the general development of its internship program.

6. The Faculty/Coordinator of the Internship Program will serve as the Internship Consultant to the agency who will:

   a. Serve as the principal liaison between the department and the agency during each academic semester.

   b. Be available for the agency as need may be concerning the relationships between the agency and the department.

   c. Make periodic visits to the agency to review the student(s) progress.

   d. Discuss policies and procedures of the Internship Course.

7. Provide opportunities for appropriate evaluations of the agency as a setting of student learning.

8. Provide a copy of the department's course syllabus.

The Agency Agrees To:

1. Accept the policy of the department that students are assigned in accordance with the provisions of the Federal Civil Rights Act.

2. Adhere to the objectives of the department as contained in its course syllabus.

3. Accept the conditions stipulated in the course syllabus.

4. Involve the students in meaningful agency programs by utilizing appropriate assignments or tasks.

5. Allow students to use their work product for academic discussion with the Faculty/Coordinator of the Internship Program.

6. Assure that each supervisor or site manager or designated representative will have adequate time within his/her work schedule to:

a. Satisfy the educational objectives of the students through development of learning opportunities.

b. Prepare for regularly scheduled conferences with students.

c. Meet with the Faculty/Coordinator of the Internship Program at periodic intervals to discuss learning opportunities and student performance.

d. Prepare reports and evaluation as required by the department.

e. Attend appropriate department sponsored meetings or conferences.

7. Permit the use of facilities by students of the department during the period of the placement, including:

a. Space for students in an area sufficiently private for carrying on the assigned work or activity.

b. Clerical services for those records and reports which are produced for the agency.

c. Access to client and agency records as they relate to agency supervision.

8. Assure that the Faculty/Coordinator of the Internship Program is advised of policy and service changes and developments which may affect student learning or the department's curriculum.

9. Inform the Faculty/Coordinator of any early or immediate problems that may develop concerning a student's progress or performance.

10. Provide reimbursement of all student travel expenses on agency business.

11. Observe the University/College calendar with respect to student holiday and vacation periods.

12. Adhere to course objectives:

a. _____

b. _____

c. _____

d. _____

e. _____

FOR THE AGENCY: FOR THE:_____

_____   UNIVERSITY OR COLLEGE AND THE

_____   DEPARTMENT

BY:_____   BY:_____

                                         FACULTY/COORDINATOR

                                         OF INTERNSHIP PROGRAM

DATE:_____   DATE:_____

APPENDIX G

INTERNSHIP SITE VISITATION REPORT

Date:_____

FIRST VISIT

Name of Student_____Title_____

Placement Area_____

Agency Evaluation of the Student Performance

Overall:

Attendance	Excellent ( )	Good ( )	Fair ( )
Reliability	Excellent ( )	Good ( )	Fair ( )
Peer Relations	Excellent ( )	Good ( )	Fair ( )
Supervisory Relations	Excellent ( )	Good ( )	Fair ( )
Understanding of Position	Excellent ( )	Good ( )	Fair ( )
Initiative	Excellent ( )	Good ( )	Fair ( )

Comments_____

_____

_____

_____

_____

SECOND VISIT

Date:_____

Name of Student_____Title_____

Placement Area_____

Agency Evaluation of the Student Performance

Overall:

Attendance	Excellent ( )	Good ( )	Fair ( )
Reliability	Excellent ( )	Good ( )	Fair ( )
Peer Relations	Excellent ( )	Good ( )	Fair ( )
Supervisory Relations	Excellent ( )	Good ( )	Fair ( )
Understanding of Position	Excellent ( )	Good ( )	Fair ( )
Initiative	Excellent ( )	Good ( )	Fair ( )

Comments_____

_____

_____

_____

_____

THIRD VISIT

Date:_____

Name of Student_____Title_____

Placement Area_____

Agency Evaluation of the Student Performance

Overall:

Attendance	Excellent ( )	Good ( )	Fair ( )
Reliability	Excellent ( )	Good ( )	Fair ( )
Peer Relations	Excellent ( )	Good ( )	Fair ( )
Supervisory Relations	Excellent ( )	Good ( )	Fair ( )
Understanding of Position	Excellent ( )	Good ( )	Fair ( )
Initiative	Excellent ( )	Good ( )	Fair ( )

Comments_____

_____

_____

_____

_____

APPENDIX H

MID-TERM REVIEW
SUPERVISOR'S EVALUATION OF STUDENT INTERN

Instruction to Student: The student must complete this portion of the evaluation form and leave it with his or her supervisor for evaluation. The supervisor should mail this evaluation to: university/college faculty/coordinator.

NAME:_____

Major_____Year_____

University/CollegeFaculty/Coordinator of
Internship:_____

Starting Date:_____Day_____Month_____Year

Ending Date:_____Day_____Month_____Year

FALL_____ SPRING_____ SUMMER_____ YEAR:_____

Name of Agency:_____

Name of Department:_____

Name of Supervisor:_____Title:_____

Normal Placement Hrs _____ to _____Total hrs/weeks_____

Description of Duties:_____

_____

_____

APPENDIX I

Itemized Projects & Tasks

The student must itemize all completed projects and tasks. The itemized list must be submitted to the supervisor.

1. _____

2. _____

3. _____

4. _____

5. _____

6. _____

7. _____

8. _____

9. _____

10. _____

APPENDIX K

FINAL REVIEW
SUPERVISOR'S EVALUATION OF STUDENT INTERN
(See Appendix K)

Instruction to Student: The student must complete this portion of the evaluation form and leave it with his or her supervisor for evaluation. The supervisor should mail this evaluation to: university/college faculty/coordinator.

NAME:_____

Major_____Year in
University/College_____

University/College Faculty/Coordinator of
Internship:_____

Starting Date:_____Day_____Month_____Year

Ending Date:_____Day_____Month_____Year

FALL_____ SPRING_____ SUMMER_____ YEAR:_____

Name of Agency:_____

Name of Department:_____

Name of Supervisor:_____ Title:_____

Normal Placement Hrs _____ to _____ Total hrs/weeks_____

Description of Duties:_____

_____

_____

_____

To be filled out by the Supervisor: The Supervisor will express an opinion of the student in the comments area. Criticisms and comments are earnestly solicited. This information will be utilized by the faculty/coordinator for the guidance of the student. You must check the appropriate box for each category

ABILITY TO LEARN

( ) Learns very quickly
( ) Learns readily
( ) Average in learning
( ) Rather slow to learn
( ) Very slow to learn

QUALITY OF WORK

( ) Excellent
( ) Very good
( ) Average
( ) Below average
( ) Very poor

ATTITUDE-APPLICATION TO WORK

( ) Outstanding in enthusiasm
( ) Very interested
( ) Average
( ) Somewhat indifferent

( ) Definitely not interested

ATTENDANCE

( ) Regular
( ) Irregular

OVERALL PERFORMANCE

( ) Outstanding
( ) Very good
( ) Average
( ) Poor

JUDGMENT

( ) Exceptionally mature
( ) Above average
( ) Makes the right decision
( ) Uses poor judgment
( ) Consistently uses bad judgment

DEPENDABILITY

( ) Completely
( ) Above average
( ) Usually dependable
( ) Sometimes neglectful
( ) Unreliable

RELATIONS WITH OTHERS

( ) Exceptionally well accepted
( ) Works well with others
( ) Gets along satisfactory
( ) Has difficulty working with others
( ) Works very poorly with others

PUNCTUALITY

( ) Regular
( ) Irregular

RESOURCES

Academy of Criminal Justice Sciences (1999). Los Angeles: Roxbury Publishing Company.

American Correctional Association (2000). Lanham, MD: .

Borzak, Lenore (ed.) (1981). Field Study: A Sourcebook of Experiential Learning. Beverly Hills, CA: Sage Publishing Company.

Brammer, L.M. (1985). The Helping Relationship: Process and Skills (3rd Ed.). Englewood Cliffs, NJ: Prentice Hall.

Goldstein A. (ed.) (1975). Practicum Manual: A Guide For Students, Faculty and Administrators. Arlington, VA: National Recreation and Park Association.

Harr, Scott J., and Hess, Karen M. (2000). Seeking Employment in Criminal Justice and Related Fields (3rd Ed.). Belmont, CA: Wadsworth Publishing Company.

Havens, L. (1976). Participant Observation. New York: J. Aronson.

Jorgensen, D.L. (1989). Participant Observation: A Methodology for Human Studies, Newbury Park, CA: Sage Publishing Company.

National Directory of Law Enforcement Administrators. (2000). Correctional Institutions and Related Agencies. Oregon, WI: Span Publishing, Inc.

Rowan University. (2001). Rowan University Career and Academic Planning. Glassboro, NJ: Rowan University.

United States Department of Justice, Law Enforcement Assistance Administration. (1968). Guideline-Participation for Internship Programs. G.5500.1A

NOTES

1. National Center For Women and Policing, (1999): p. 9

2. Ibid., p.10

3. National Directory of Law Enforcement Administrators, (2000): pp. 1-248

4. Harr, Scott J., Seeking Employment in Criminal Justice and Related Fields, (2000): p. 159

5. Sanchez-Leguelinel, Caridad, Wadsworth's Guide to Careers in Criminal Justice, (1999): p. 59

6. Ibid.

7. Ibid., p. 49

8. Ibid., p. 42

9. Ibid., p. 42

10. Ibid., p. 43

11. Ibid., p. 43

12. American Correctional Association, (2000): pp. 55-695

13. National Directory of Law Enforcement Administrators, (2000): pp. 844-847, 856, 873-878

14. Wadsworth's Guide to Careers in Criminal Justice, (1999): p. 38

15. Academy of Criminal Justice Sciences, (1999): pp. 1-213.

INDEX

CPSIA information can be obtained at www.ICGtesting.com
Printed in the USA
LVOW02s0247040715

444476LV00003B/5/P